Endorsements

In *Building an Elite Career*, Don provides the ultimate road-map to success and happiness, showing life is meant to be lived like a marathon, not a sprint, and in doing so, with the right strategy and discipline, you can create the habits that propel you to build an extraordinary life.

Charlie Engle
Ultra-Marathon Runner, Keynote Speaker & Author of
Running Man

Don does it again! As the author of *Exponential Theory*, I recognize the potential of transformative ideas, and the importance of crafting an extraordinary life marked by intentionality, happiness, and success to thrive in entrepreneurial organizations. Don Wenner has achieved that and more, presenting a blueprint for prosperity and fulfillment that will enable readers to make a lasting impact on the world."

Aaron Bare
Wall Street Journal Bestselling Author

Awesome! In *Building an Elite Career*, Don gives us the playbook to stop living by default and start living by design. That's what it's all about, right? To live with intentionality and in alignment with our values is at the core of this book and there's no one that practices that better than Don. Don has done it again with this book and I can't recommend it highly enough.

Trav Bell
World's No.1 Bucket List Expert
Keynote Speaker, Best Selling Author

BUILDING AN ELITE CAREER

BUILDING AN ELITE CAREER

THE BLUEPRINT TO THRIVING IN A HIGH-GROWTH ORGANIZATION

DON WENNER

Published by Ethos Collective™
PO Box 43, Powell, OH 43065
Ethoscollective.vip

Identifiers:

LCCN:2023904880
Paperback ISBN:978-1-63680-140-7
Hardback ISBN: 978-1-63680-141-4
eBook ISBN: 978-1-63680-142-1

Available in paperback, hardback, e-book, and audiobook.

CONTENTS

SECTION 4: UTILIZING EES TO DRIVE PRODUCTIVITY

FOREWORD

It's relatively easy to make a living, but more difficult to make a life. *Building an Elite Career* is the synthesis of simple, actionable ideas and disciplines that will enable you and me to move beyond just having a successful career to having a successful life supported by a great career.

Imagine if, in the end, your life produced 100x. In other words, you invested the time, energy, skill, and influence you were given or gained with such focus and leverage that the results multiplied 100 times. What impact would you want to see from your life? What would that feel like? What would the experience be of those who worked for and with you and of those you loved?

Peter Drucker used to ask the simple but profound question of those he mentored "To what end?" In other words, what would the purpose be, or perhaps more specifically, what is your purpose? Why would you want your life to be 100x extraordinary?

Don and I are on a journey together to live 100x lives. The difference is I'm in my 60s, and he's in his 30s, and that is precisely why the wisdom in this book is unique—Don has figured out how to live a 100x life in the most intense season of life. We are not the most talented people on the planet or the most winsome, and we don't have the deepest faith, but we are growing, and as a result, I can already see Don producing 100x impact, and he has many decades ahead, God willing.

I have spent the last three decades inspiring, coaching, and equipping successful leaders who find themselves at an inflection point, having built successful careers but longing for more meaning, joy, and impact. The sad part is that they could have had both at the same time if they had learned the skills and simple practices you will find in this book.

There are lots of great leadership books, most written by older leaders deep into their careers, having paid a steep price for their success. Many have sacrificed intimacy with their spouse, time with their kids, meaningful friendships, and perhaps their health along the way.

What is unique about this book is that Don is young and has been highly successful in his career without sacrificing an intimate relationship with his wife Carla, their three little boys, friends, his health, or the compassionate impact he wants to make in thousands of lives through affordable housing and philanthropy.

The two questions you want to ask yourself as you begin this book are, "What is all my 'career winning' costing me?" and "Am I willing to learn new career skills so that I don't sacrifice priceless things in pursuit of things that are merely valuable?"

Take notes as you move through this book and put the most important new disciplines into your calendar as regular practices. Looking back 30 years from now, you will be blown away by the compounding impact you will have by building an elite career as the foundation for a truly great life.

Lloyd Reeb, Founding Partner of the Halftime Institute
and author of *From Success to Significance:*
When the Pursuit of Success Isn't Enough

SECTION I

ELITE EXECUTION SYSTEM

INTRODUCTION

Being part of an organization that is growing at a dramatic pace is an exhilarating experience. The constant expansion of ideas and prospects in such companies creates tremendous potential for you to make an impact on others and to grow personally and professionally. The opportunities to take leadership and drive results are endless—*if* you are ready to accept them.

To be ready, you first need to understand how to work in a high-growth, entrepreneurial environment. You must also possess the confidence that you can positively impact that growth and consistently drive results. All of this requires a firm grasp of the organization's systems, mission, and goals. Without that foundation, the experience of working in such a fast-paced arena can be overwhelming—exhausting and frustrating—and leave you struggling to make an impact.

Building an Elite Career will give the framework, guidelines, and tools necessary to thrive in a growing entrepreneurial organization. You'll learn how to make a significant and positive difference in the company you work for. Equally as important, this book will equip you to grow and prosper in *all* areas of your life.

My journey to writing this book started more than thirty years ago with my first entrepreneurial venture. I was in first grade when I saw an opportunity. One day, my father added Hostess® doughnuts—the little chocolate ones that come six to a pack—to my lunch bag. My classmates, who were stuck with graham crackers, apples, or other less appealing desserts, were envious of those treats. Then it hit me: I could sell the doughnuts for fifty cents apiece! They would be happy, and I would make a little money.

Dad must have thought I really loved doughnuts, because I began asking him to pack them for my lunch every day. Armed with a supply of mini chocolate doughnuts and no overhead or expenses—at least none to me—I cleared a cool three dollars on every pack of doughnuts. Not bad for a six-year-old in 1990.

My business was short-lived—the school found out what was going on, told my parents, and my supply chain disappeared—but that sweet taste of success set me on the path of entrepreneurship and hard work. That path continued with my lawn mowing business in middle school and into high school. In college, I worked at several jobs, primarily in restaurants, and learned a little more about how businesses operate.

My mindset has always been that *if someone else can do it, so can I.* From an early age, I believed that if I had an example to follow and was willing to learn and work hard, I could do anything. So when a financial advisor spoke to my eighth-grade class on career day, inspiration hit again. This time, the potential income was far more than selling doughnuts in the lunchroom. While he was speaking, he flashed a chart on the screen that listed earnings for doctors, lawyers, accountants, engineers, and, of course, financial advisors. His chosen career path out earned all the others. The numbers got my attention, and when he said that to succeed as a financial advisor, you had to be self-motivated and good at math, I was hooked.

Wow, I can do that. I am good at math and self-motivated. My young mind whirred with possibilities.

Determined to learn more about the career, I shadowed several financial advisors that summer. I would show up with a long list of questions and take tons of notes. The more I learned about their jobs, the more convinced I became that if the advisors I met could be successful, so could I.

As soon as I turned eighteen, I received insurance and securities licenses and began interviewing for firms to work for—until I was presented with a different opportunity. At the age of nineteen, as a college student studying finance at Drexel University and planning to become a financial advisor, I was waiting tables at Texas Roadhouse on the weekends to earn money to pay for college and my living expenses. (I had moved out on my own while I was still in high school.) It was there that a customer named Nathan Robinson convinced me to come work for him in his ADT Security business. I knew absolutely nothing about security systems, but Nathan told me that the average skilled sales associate earned $2,000 a week.

I reasoned that if others were making $2,000 per week, there was no reason I couldn't do it as well. I knew I would work as hard as anyone and that I could learn anything. My first paycheck was $5,218 for two weeks. I earned $6,000 to $8,000 every two weeks thereafter in that job. Although still a full-time college student, I became the number one sales representative in the country in less than six months—out of about 100,000 sales representatives. Years later, I found out that, until I went to work for him, Nathan had never had a sales rep on his team who earned $2,000 per week. From the start, however, he instilled that expectation in me, which was one of the keys to my success.

While attending Drexel, I also took classes at the local community college so I could earn more credits per semester and decrease the cost of my education (I would max out the allowable credits at Drexel of 18 to 20 and take another 10 to 15 credits at the community college). The added class load, however, was not an excuse or a reason to lower my expectations or efforts. It simply required more discipline, more focus, and more intentional activity.

One Friday night, when I was twenty years old, I was at Nathan's house, and he was writing me my check for the past two weeks' commissions. It had been a great two weeks, and I had earned around $7,000. I was happy to pick up that check, but a check for $17,000 on Nathan's table caught my eye. It was his earnings from his other job as real estate agent at Keller Williams Real Estate.

Right away, I began peppering him with questions about real estate. We hadn't talked long when he told me he thought I would do great selling real estate and that he would teach me the business. Up until that point, my plan was to finish college and become a financial advisor. After giving it a great deal of thought for a few weeks, I decided I was in. I gave up sleep for a few weeks, earned my real estate license, and took off. While still selling alarm systems to pay my bills, I focused on selling real estate—prospecting, knocking on doors, showing houses, and working hard to sell homes. I knew that there were more than one million real estate agents across the country doing the same job but only a small percentage of them were truly successful.

Again, I wondered: *If someone else could do it, why couldn't I?* I could and I did.

My point in sharing this part of my story is to help you see that *you* can, and *you* will do what you set out to achieve *if* you are willing to learn and work with purpose and focused effort. In short, you can have an elite career. Using the system outlined in this book, I believe you can reach the goals you want to achieve in your career and your personal life.

I've come a long way since my first few years in real estate. I founded DLP Capital, a private real estate investment and financial services firm focused on creating prosperity and making an impact by investing in communities. We help make housing affordable and devote efforts to relieving the job crisis. Through our elite membership community, prosperity community, and by lending and partnering with housing developers, builders, and operators, we are helping people create strong legacies and experience a better quality of life. We provide investment funds that serve thousands of families—primarily faith-centered wealth creators—and provide development, construction, portfolio management, insurance, and closing services to maximize our impact.

Over the years, DLP has flourished for several reasons, and one of the most important is that my team and I developed and actively use the Elite Execution System (EES) to plan for, support, and execute growth toward our goals. EES is a proven system that supports and drives organizational and individual achievement of goals that simply would not be possible without the system.

DLP has been able to 10X our revenue every five years since 2006 because we have incredible team members who have learned the principles shared in this book and leverage the Elite Execution System to achieve their personal goals and the goals of the company.

Why Read *Building an Elite Career?*

I wrote my previous book, *Building an Elite Organization*, for other entrepreneurs. I wanted to show others how to develop a comprehensive system, tailored for their companies, that would allow them to scale their successful businesses more rapidly. That book shared how I, along with my team, developed the system that has allowed us to grow an average of 60 percent each year since 2006.

I wrote *Building an Elite Career* for people like you who have joined an organization that uses the Elite Execution System. It's designed to give you a better understanding of what the company is doing, why it is being done, and how it is being done. Most importantly, it provides you with a blueprint to prosperity, happiness, and fulfillment so you can make a bigger impact on the world around you through both your personal and professional success. Even if you are not part of an organization running EES, you can use this book to build an elite career; and who knows, maybe bringing EES to your organization may be a tremendous way for you to make a significant impact on your organization.

If you are like me and most other driven individuals, you read or listen to inspirational books, attend events or conferences, and listen to podcasts. You might even listen to our podcast, *Don Wenner's Elite Impact Podcast.* With so many amazing role models to learn from, it is easy to jump from one idea to the next.

This is where the Elite Execution System comes in. As you go through this book, you might recognize some of the ideas and tools. It is literally the best-of concepts from or inspired by some of the great business and personal growth thought leaders in the world.

Since launching my company, I have used this system to build and grow DLP—and improve many areas of my personal life. Through trial and error, practice, and evaluation, my team and I have refined and improved EES to make it an effective and encompassing operating system that you can use to create success and experience fulfillment in all aspects of life.

Throughout this book, you'll see references to free downloads and resources designed to help you apply what you've learned. You can access all of these at DLPElite.com/resources, or scan the QR code:

If you are ready to learn the system that will help you thrive and prosper in your career and throughout life, please, read on.

CHAPTER 1

THE ELITE EXECUTION SYSTEM

A culture of discipline involves a duality. On the one hand, it requires people who adhere to a consistent system; yet, on the other hand, it gives people freedom and responsibility within the framework of that system.

—Jim Collins, *Good to Great: Why Some Companies Make the Leap . . . and Others Don't*

Discipline. **Structure. Accountability.** These words typically don't bring up thoughts of happiness or excitement, do they? But it's these three practices that lay the foundation for big goal achievement.

That said, you likely know (or know about) entrepreneurial-minded individuals who are self-driven and passionate, who value their own independence, and who even adopt a rules-are-meant-to-be-broken attitude. They reject the idea of accountability.

At first glance, you might agree with their attitude. The standard definition of *accountable* from Dictionary.com is to be "subject to having to report, explain or justify; responsible; answerable." That doesn't sound very enjoyable; I understand.

Even if that kind of attitude and disregard for discipline and structure yields short-term reward, it takes its toll over time.

Those who succeed in all aspects of life know that discipline that lies at the center of their success. Maybe it's time for a paradigm shift in the way we think about these words. *The Oz Principle*, a book authored by Craig Hickman, Roger Connors, and Tom Smith, offers an alternative definition for accountability: "*a personal choice to rise above one's circumstances and demonstrate the ownership necessary for achieving desired results.*" That sounds a bit better, doesn't it? And a whole lot more empowering because it's a choice.

Maybe the traits of discipline, structure, and accountability come easily to you. If you're like many people, you have to work at them. Regardless of how natural they feel right now, the framework provided by the Elite Execution System will empower you to develop these traits and use them to your advantage. As you harness their power and apply them within EES, you'll see a change. You'll begin to thrive in business and life and will have the ability to make even greater contributions to the success of your team, family, and community.

When all the members of an organization choose to follow the principles of EES, they achieve more in ninety days than most achieve in a year.

When you develop discipline—learning to establish and commit to consistent routines, habits, and meeting schedules—you become free to innovate, create, and focus on what is most important. The consistent rhythms you put into action ensure that you keep the ball moving forward in all the key areas of business and life. You'll also gain the mental freedom to focus the rest of your time and energy around what is most impactful and exciting now.

Without a system like EES, it can feel like you have an endless number of competing priorities at work and in life.

Ensuing feelings of chaos and confusion can lead to inaction or to focusing only on what is most urgent, which is not necessarily the best course of action. Several years ago I realized this: *Urgent things are usually not that important.* That feels counterintuitive. When you are faced with completing a transaction, solidifying a deal, or addressing an issue that is happening in real time, you feel at that moment like it is the most important thing in the world. But the reality is that urgent priorities—the whirlwind—are rarely what are *most* important. In addition, what is most important is rarely urgent.

Another way to think about this is that urgent priorities *act upon you*, whereas the most important priorities are those *you must act upon*.

If you are anything like me, and you turn to the wisdom of business and personal development gurus for insights, it can be tempting to chase after that *one thing* that will enable you to achieve incredible success. The problem is, that one thing could be a million different things: being a better leader, getting more organized, learning content marketing, becoming a great storyteller, improving management skills, or hiring the best people.

The reality, though, is that there is no magic bullet for success in business or in life. In fact, if you put all your focus on just one area of business or life, you will likely end up with even more obstacles and challenges.

To build an elite career, it is important to understand that every organization has four key quadrants or components. Each of these quadrants must work together, as part of one overarching plan, for the organization to generate consistent growth and profitability.

Four Quadrants

The four quadrants of the Elite Execution System are strategy, people, operations, and acceleration. Each of these are well-defined, with activities, principles, and actions that create a continuous cycle of growth.

THE 4 QUADRANTS
of the Elite Execution System

Strategy	**People**	**Operations**	**Acceleration**
What, Where, When Disciplined Thoughts	Who Disciplined People	Execution of the How Disciplined Action	How Disciplined Action

Source: DLP Capital

Strategy

Strategy is the *why* and *what* of the quadrant.

According to Jim Collins, author of one of my favorite books, *Great by Choice*, strategy comes from disciplined thought. The unexpected truth is that it doesn't take a lot of disciplined thought to come up with great ideas. Great ideas are a dime a dozen. Growing an organization requires saying *no* to great ideas more often than saying *yes*.

The real qualification of being a good strategist is having the discernment to select the *right* great ideas—the ones that are ripe for and worthy of execution. It's the ability to evaluate all the ideas, possibilities, and different paths of growth and select the best of the best on which to focus one's resources.

An excellent strategist will consider what, where, and when. Then, employing focused, disciplined thought, the strategist will determine the optimal course.

With that in mind, don't be disheartened if the great ideas you shared in meetings aren't the ideas that are selected for immediate action. It doesn't mean your idea wasn't valuable. It simply means that there were other ideas that were more suited for execution *at that time*.

People

I consider the second quadrant, people, (or *who*) to be the most critical of the Elite Execution System. And when I say "people," I am including you.

The bottom-line truth is that leaders—no matter how talented, skilled, knowledgeable, or well-funded—cannot possibly do everything on their own. Even if time weren't an issue, successful leaders must build teams that help them balance their many different skills and strengths.

It's essential to attract, develop, and retain great people (that's you!). Team members are selected not only because they have the skills necessary for the role but also because they fit into the organization's culture, share the company's values, and are willing and able to perform the job at the needed level.

In the Elite Execution System, these people are called Rock Star A Players. (Remember, that's you!) And within EES, each person has very clear expectations or results that that person is responsible to achieve. The ownership of key outcomes or expectations by each person in the organization is at the center of the people quadrant and is central to the success of the entire organization.

Think of the company where you work. When it started, the founder or another key leader likely had to perform your role. Eventually those duties were delegated to you. Now it's your responsibility to exhibit the discipline and commitment necessary to pull together your own team to carry out your organization's winning strategy.

Operations

The third quadrant, operations, is *how* members of the organization implement and execute the strategy to achieve the goals set for the organization's growth. Each operation is executed with a strategy that addresses the risks, both internal and external, facing the business.

As each operation is executed, the employee and his or her leader measure its effectiveness. The Elite Execution System's most important metrics are related to the performance of our team members. That's why such focus is given to defining each team member's role, responsibilities, expectations, and key numbers (RREKs), which we'll discuss at length in a later chapter, as well as their quarterly goals (Rocks), which must be specific, measurable, achievable, relevant, and time-bound (SMART).

With clear standards and well-defined goals, you can move forward with confidence, knowing you're devoting time and attention to the things that are most important to your role and most crucial to the company's success. Rocks have a built-in accountability system that clearly indicates if you are "on track" or "off track" on the progress to meet your goal. Another part of EES that creates a cadence of accountability is Wildly Important Goals (WIGs), which involve the team working together to accomplish one goal. Again, we'll dive into the details of Rocks and WIGs later in the book.

Don't let the concept of accountability intimidate you. While it can generate negative connotations, accountability within the Elite Execution System simply means you'll account for your ability regarding your responsibilities and expectations.

Other aspects of the operations quadrant include how to hold productive meetings, how to stay organized and aligned for maximum productivity, and how to gather the tools necessary to enhance your execution. Using this system requires discipline, which makes disciplined people the key to successful operations.

Acceleration

Acceleration is about how the company scales its revenue through a cohesive approach that involves sales and marketing working together. This requires disciplined action in the communication throughout the company.

For acceleration to occur, there must be a disciplined system to grow the brand. Organizations must clearly define what they offer, differentiate themselves from the competition, and leverage sales and marketing to scale and accelerate the business.

An important part of acceleration is the effort of each team member to "deliver wow" and contribute to an exceptional customer experience.

Acceleration is achieved only when you and your team members can consistently accomplish each of these tasks.

Succeeding with the Elite Execution System

The best part of the Elite Execution System is how it clarifies your priorities, breaks down large tasks into smaller ones, and enables you to track your progress. This means you can immediately know what your focus needs to be for the day, week, and month.

Of course, achieving success will require personal energy and effort. If you aren't accustomed to daily tracking, it may take practice to develop the habit. But the systems and structures within the Elite Execution System—the Compass, accountability of Rocks and Milestones, the WIGs and meetings, and even the frequency of communication with your leader—are all in place to keep you focused on what is truly most important and to ensure that the company's growth isn't outstripping its processes. These systems and structures allow your company to scale much more efficiently than it might if you generated an out-of-control sales explosion and found yourself scrambling to keep up with the results.

Discipline

At this point, you might be thinking that systems, structure, and process are still not all that exciting. You might want to close this book and go back to the way you have always done things.

We all have different levels of talents, skills, and cognitive abilities that can carry us to success. If you are completely satisfied with your life and career and have no interest in growing, improving, or moving into an elite role, you might be reading the wrong book, and you might be in the wrong organization. But if you desire excellence and the chance to move to the next level in your career, the Elite Execution System will provide you with the systems, structure, and rhythm necessary to achieve elite levels of results in your career and in your life.

I believe it is my responsibility to maximize the gifts, blessings, and opportunities the Lord has provided me. That means living a disciplined life and making the commitment to sacrifice what I want in the moment for greater impact in the long run.

Traits of Successful Team Members

Organizations utilizing EES are led by entrepreneurial leaders. These leaders are passionate, driven, and goal-oriented. They spend a significant amount of their time pressing toward the company's Big Hairy Audacious Goal (BHAG). (More on that later.)

Every leader has an individual style; some will be more formal, some innately casual. To be optimally effective, learn the communication style of your leaders and mirror it to them. Strong and clear communication lines are critical for success in an elite organization. This might come naturally in some relationships but will take more work in other cases. The investment of time and effort to build real relationships will pay dividends towards achieving elite results. We will talk through some tools and best practices to achieve these results in the chapters ahead.

Driven leaders of elite organizations are often "High A" personalities, individuals who are primarily results oriented and comfortable moving at a fast pace. They value team members who can present clear facts and information. They also want innovative team members who will commit to understanding and researching a company-wide problem, think deeply about the options, and offer a proven solution.

As a new member on any team, it is critical to understand how a leader prefers to communicate so you can quickly bring value to the team and be able to best collaborate. The most successful team members in elite organizations are those who are proactive and who leverage the Elite Execution System to drive results. They consistently bring forward issues and solutions. They show up to each meeting prepared and embrace the adage, "Many have the will to win, but few have the will to prepare to win." They also bring high energy and positivity to each interaction and opportunity.

CHAPTER 2

THE ELITE COMPASS

Knowing where you are going is the first step to getting there.

—Ken Blanchard

To be a contributor to a high-growth business, you need clear direction. The Elite Compass is the organization's roadmap or plan with a clear vision and strategy to define where the company is going and includes the One-Year Bull's-eye, the Three-Year Aim, and the Big Hairy Audacious Goal (BHAG). While the Elite Compass is for an organization, you'll also be able to design your own Personal Compass for achieving individual goals, which we will cover later.

The Elite Compass provides a bird's-eye view of the company, captures its values, defines its purpose, and maps out its mission. The leaders of your organization utilize the Elite Compass and update it each year with a timetable for aligning objectives, assessing progress, and achieving goals.

For elite organizations, this compass is not what an organization hopes to accomplish or thinks it can do or will do if everything goes well. It is what the organization *will* accomplish regardless of the things that will go wrong and despite what external challenges the company faces. The Elite Compass is a living document that is typically updated annually. Elite organizations seek feedback, ideas, and participation from the team members throughout the organization in creating and updating the compass each year.

At DLP, we engage our team members via surveys and through strategy sessions, typically in early- to mid-fourth quarter every year. This is when we draft the One-Year Bull's-eye for the upcoming year, update the Three-Year Aim, and review and adjust other areas of the compass as needed.

Become familiar with your organization's compass as soon as possible. Simply put, if you want to have an elite career, you must make a direct impact on achieving the goals of your organization, and the best way to do that is using the compass to drive your focus and efforts.

As I walk you through some of the key components of the Elite Compass, note that not all organizations have developed all these areas yet. Younger companies might still be developing their compasses.

Core Values

Core values are more than just words on a piece of paper. They differentiate a company from the competition. They determine the kinds of employees who are hired, how clients are served, and how the organization grows. Core values are so intrinsic to the company that the actions and decisions of teams across the organization should align with them.

Often, a company's core values are developed over several years. Senior leaders review them regularly to ensure they reflect the entire organization. There is no set number of core values, though some consider ten to be high. An accepted, best practice is to have between four and eight.

As an example, here are DLP's core values and how we define each of them:

- **Driven for Greatness**—We are driven to seek knowledge and pursue growth and greatness each day in both our personal and professional lives.
- **Servant Leadership**—We influence and impact our community, clients, and ourselves by exemplifying integrity, positivity, and humble confidence.
- **Grit (Passion & Perseverance for Long-term Goals)**—We have the endurance and unshakable commitment necessary to achieve our visionary long-term goals.
- **Enthusiastically Delivering WOW!**—We go above and beyond, delighting and amazing everyone we encounter.
- **Living Fully**—Our quest for excellence and the pursuit of our passions applies to all aspects of our lives—business, family, personal, and faith. We strive to live life to the fullest.
- **Innovative Solution Focus**—We do not simply talk about problems; we drive ourselves to create solutions that produce new, previously-thought-to-be-unimaginable results for our clients.
- **Twenty-Mile March**—We consistently hit targets, day after day, year after year, regardless of the prevailing conditions.
- **Execution & Excellence**—We establish and surpass expectations that can only be achieved through a clear focus, commitment, and engagement on completing the most critical priorities.
- **Humble Confidence**—We exude confidence without arrogance, projecting humility and warmth to empower others and emphasize collaboration.

- **Stewardship**—We are maximizing the resources entrusted to us to deliver positive returns.

It is not possible for you to have an elite career within your company if your behaviors do not fully align with the core values. Note: There is no "usually" to my statement. This is absolute. If you are not aligned, either you need to change, the organization needs to change—which could only be possible if you are a senior leader—or you need to find a role in a new organization.

Tagline

Our company has several strengths, things that give us an advantage over the competition, and so does yours. The core values, purpose, and mission all help you know what your company stands for. Something else that will help you understand a company more fully is its tagline—the phrase that's so important that it acts as a summary for the public.

At DLP, our tagline is *Building Thriving Communities and Transforming Lives*. Be sure to learn your organization's tagline so you can quickly express the most important facets the public should know.

Brand Promises

Your brand promises are the things that people know they can expect when they do business with you. These are not shallow marketing statements. These are the deeply ingrained in your corporate reputation, often established over years and decades, that the public expects consciously or subconsciously when they work with your company.

As an example, at DLP, our first brand promise is efficiency or speed. Our clients know they are going to get fast results from us consistently. They know we will be able to close quickly and perform efficiently. If they need to get a deal done under the gun, they know they can count on DLP.

Our second brand promise has to do with our ability to execute—our guaranteed results. When clients engage with us to sell their homes, secure a loan for them, or provide a safe rental property to live in, they will get exactly what we promise to give them. We show up every time, and we guarantee results.

Our third brand promise is to provide a "Wow!" experience. People know that we are going to make every interaction as enjoyable as possible. This applies across all DLP's businesses, every time.

As a team member, it is critical to make sure your activities are aligned with your organization's brand promises.

Purpose (The Why)

For an organization to be elite, that company must have an inspiring purpose. A purpose is your company's *why*—why it does what it does. This purpose should be inspiring to the team members who work for the organization and for their clients or customers.

One of the biggest crises in America is what we call the *happiness crisis*, which is derived from people having a lack of connection. People often look for connection in the wrong places, such as social media. I believe that the first place we need to look to for connection is with God. In my experience, nothing can replace or be substituted for a relationship with God. In addition to a strong relationship with the Lord, a connection to a purpose on earth—to something bigger than oneself—is essential. One of the greatest human desires is to feel useful and that we belong to a larger community. When humans have purpose, they can be inspired and motivated to do amazing things.

At DLP, our purpose is: *Dream. Live. Prosper. Passionately making an extraordinary impact by transforming lives and building thriving communities.*

Mission (The What)

A company's mission shows what the company is going to accomplish in order to live out their purpose. The purpose is inspirational, while the mission is actionable.

For example, although DLP's purpose statement certainly inspires, it does not convey action. Our mission statement, however, proposes a clear plan:

To become the largest investor in rental housing communities and resorts in the world.

We display this mission statement on our website, in our marketing materials, and in all our job ads. When people interact with a DLP team member, we want them to know and feel that we are dedicated to fulfilling our mission every day.

Your leaders selected you to be a part of an elite organization because the hiring team believes you can help the company achieve its mission.

One-Year Bull's-Eye

Your company's Elite Compass includes what the business will focus on and achieve within the next year. (Personally, this is my favorite part of the Elite Compass.) The One-Year Bull's-eye has between four and ten key numbers.

Key numbers are vital, but why track so aggressively? Think of it this way: When leaders are keeping score, people are engaged, and they play or work much harder.

Have you ever watched a group of kids playing a casual game of basketball? If no one is keeping score, the pace is relaxed and there will be good-natured laughter at mistakes and half-hearted cheers at baskets made. When someone—a player or a bystander—starts keeping score, the atmosphere changes. The pace picks up, and there's now an intensity (and possibly an elbow) that wasn't there before.

By keeping score—or rather, keeping track of key numbers—you'll notice that everyone "ups their game" and produces stronger growth. These metrics let you know how close you are to meeting your short- and long-term goals, and they help you adjust your activity as needed. Specific people, not a larger team, own key numbers and are responsible for meeting or increasing them. These are numbers that might include revenue, profit, number of clients, number of employees, or any other key measurement.

For DLP, the Key Numbers in our One-Year Bull's-eye as the following:

Key Numbers:
PPP: $630,000
Deal Financed via DLP Funds: $1.2 billion
Deals Closed via non DLP Funds debt: $1.2 billion
Deals closed with DLP as owner: $600 million/ $250MM equity deployed
Capital Raised: $600 million
Yield on cost %: 7.0%
Fund Yield- Actual to Budget: 110%
Portfolio Wide NOI Target: >100%
Percentage of A Players: 80%
WACC: 8.00%
People we provide Housing to: 100,000
Lives Impacted: 400,000
Revenue $: $500,000,000
AUM $: $5,000,000,000
EUM $: $1,750,000,000
Ground up Units/rentable pads complete: 1,200

From there, we laid out a very clear plan to achieve these goals, with all team members not only knowing the clear vision but also being inspired to be a part of reaching these goals.

The compass states clear goals for each of the four quadrants of the Elite Execution System: strategy, operations, accelerations, and people. Some of these goals on an organization's compass are stretch goals, which means they are going to be difficult to achieve. It is going to require consistent focus and execution all year long from you and your team to achieve them, but they are attainable. These are not big, lofty goals that would be nice to achieve but rather the organization-wide commitments that will involve consistent focus to achieve.

The One-Year Bull's-eye has top goals that will move the business forward this year in achieving the mission, goals that would get you closer to the Three-Year Aim, keep you on track to the organization's Seven-Year Checkpoints, and keep you moving toward achieving the BHAG.

Each of the key goals for the organization's One-Year Bull's-eye must be owned by one person and one person only. This is the person with whom the "buck stops" in terms of achieving that specific goal. That goal should become one of the top expectations for that team member and added to that team member's RREK (role, responsibilities, expectation, and key numbers), which we will cover later. Every team member in the organization owns goals or has expectations that directly contribute to achieving the One-Year Bull's-eye.

If you do not currently own any of the top goals of the One-Year Bull's-eye, you should be making sure that what you do "own" is aligned with the goals of your organization. In addition, if you are serious about building an elite career, you should aspire to own some of the top goals of your company and make this goal known to your leader.

Rocks (Ninety-Day Actions)

The Elite Execution System divides One-Year Bull's-eyes into ninety-day increments. These ninety-day Rocks list the actions necessary to achieve your one-year goals, allowing you to drill further down into execution by starting with action. It is exciting to start every quarter with the realization that you are going to accomplish more in the quarter ahead than the competition will accomplish all year.

We are going to cover these quarterly, action-based goal-setting tools, called Rocks and Milestones, in detail in Chapter 15.

Three-Year Aim

A Three-Year Aim is what the company is going to "look like" in three years, and it is designed to give richness and clarity to the direction of the organization. It should be as vivid as possible.

A Three-Year Aim starts with the top four to ten key numbers of the organization, with a target for each number three years from now. In addition to your key numbers, your company's Three-Year Aim contains your big three goals that are non-negotiable. These are goals that you will 100 percent make sure you accomplish despite other things that might change over the next three years. For DLP, these three are:

1. $3 Billion Fund Manager
2. $7.5 Billion AUM
3. 13 Years on Inc. 5000 List

Companies that use EES usually include as much detail as possible regarding what the company will look like, where it will operate, where the offices are, who the clients are, and what will be accomplished. The Three-Year Aim is expressed as Key Numbers as well. For example, DLP's are the following:

PPP: $1,000,000
Deals Financed via DLP Funds: $2.4 billion
Deals Closed via non DLP Funds debt: $2.4 billion
Deals closed with DLP as owner: $1.2 billion / $400 mm equity
Capital Raised: $1 billion
Yield on cost %: 7.5%
Fund Yield- Actual to Budget: 105%
Portfolio Wide NOI Target: > 100%
Percentage of A Players:85%
WACC: 7%
People we provide Housing to: 150,000
Lives Impacted: 600,000
Revenue $: $700,000,000
AUM $: $7,500,000,000
EUM $: $3,000,000,000
Ground up Units/rentable pads complete: 2,400

Big Hairy Audacious Goal (BHAG)

Closely connected to your mission is your BHAG. The name comes from Jim Collins's book *Good to Great*. Jim refers to a company's overarching goal—the one that would help it achieve the ultimate success—the Big Hairy Audacious Goal or BHAG (pronounced *bee-hag*).

Every single team member has a vital part to play in helping the company achieve the BHAG.

How big, hairy, and audacious are BHAGs in reality?

At DLP, our BHAG is "Provide housing to 1 million people, and positively impact and transform 10 million lives leading to a spot on the Forbes list of top 100 private companies in America."

Strategy Statement

The Strategy Statement communicates what a company is going to accomplish in the years to come. It's an awesome way of articulating the compass in an action-oriented "affirmation" crafted to inspire and motivate everyone involved with the organization's current and future success.

For example, a company's strategy statement might include any of these pronouncements:

- "We are going to deliver on our brand promise of speed, execution, and delivering wow."
- "Our elite membership community will be the largest owner of housing in America."
- "We will be known as the best direct real estate lender in the country."

The strategy statement typically starts with large goals:

- "We will originate $4 billion in deals."
- "We will achieve our annual theme of 'Bigger, Better, Faster,' doubling our average deal size this year."

Leaders of organizations using EES will often share this statement with team members as part of Vision Day, or a similar presentation where the leader shares the vision with the organization. These often create great excitement about the future and serve as a guide for existing team members and as a recruiting tool for prospective team members who would want to be a part of this vision.

Core Client

The core client is the archetype of the person organizations are in business to serve. This is the person organizations think about when they create products and design services. For example, DLP's core client is a principal or owner with $10 million in net worth and a desire to invest in housing.

It's important to know who your company's core client is so that you consistently tailor your actions and activities to serve that group of people.

Secret Weapon

A secret weapon is a company's unique differentiator, the magic sauce, the thing that sets it apart from the competition in such a significant way that it ensures continued growth and success.

For example, while it might be easy for us at DLP to think our secret weapons are the products and services we offer or even our commitment to "Wow!" experiences, this is not the case. DLP's secret weapon is our adoption of the Twenty-Mile March, an approach to strategic discipline. In fact, the Twenty-Mile March is such an integral aspect of our operating system that I have incorporated it into the Elite Execution System and recommend that all Elite companies adopt it. We will talk more about the Twenty-Mile March in Chapter 14.

Key Leaders

The key leaders of your company are those on the leadership team who identify and then help the company be congruent with its purpose, mission, and core values. Far from being sequestered in an ivory tower, key leaders of a company using the Elite Execution System are connected with their team members. They are engaged weekly in accountability (both to each other and towards their teams) and are active mentors. Engagement with key leaders is necessary and encouraged; they help guide and redirect when plans are off track. Know who your key leader is, as well as their preferred method and style of communication.

The Flywheel

The Flywheel concept, popularized by Jim Collins, is the idea that there is no one single defining action that leads to an organization's success, but rather, an overall process that resembles relentlessly pushing a heavy flywheel. It will be slow at first, but as you continue to push, you build momentum and strength.

For an example of DLP's flywheel, examine the diagram below:

GROWTH FLYWHEEL

1. **Capital Invested**
Building legacies, families, and wealth for faith-centered wealth creators.

2. **Invested in Housing**
Through debt and equity for elite housing operators, developers, and builders.

4. **Create Prosperity**
For residents, team members, investors, and operators by helping people live fully and build elite careers and lives.

3. **Build Elite Organizations**
Scaling companies through the Elite Execution: both DLP Capital and the operators with whom we invest.

1. CAPITAL INVESTED

2. INVESTING IN HOUSING

3. BUILD ELITE ORGANIZATIONS

4. CREATE PROSPERITY

dlp capital

Source: DLP Capital

The Hedgehog Concept

Likewise, Jim Collins developed the Hedgehog Concept in his book *Good to Great*. He describes it as "a simple, crystalline concept that flows from deep understanding about the intersection of the following three circles": 1) what you are deeply passionate about, 2) what you can be the best in the world at, and 3) what best drives your economic or resource engine.

Transformations from good to great come about by a series of good decisions made consistently with a Hedgehog Concept, supremely well executed, accumulating one upon another, over a long period of time. By understanding the Hedgehog Concept, you have crystal clarity for the strategy and direction of your business.

Key Revenue Drivers

As a Rock Star A Player, you need to understand what drives results and revenue for your organization and, more specifically, the division for which you work. Being aware of the products and services offered that are most critical to growth, revenue, and profits helps maintain focus on action items that affect these areas.

One of our key revenue drivers at DLP is adding new, elite members to our elite community—value-aligned housing developers, builders, and operators who have already achieved success but want to scale their business and make a significant impact.

Be sure to find out what the key revenue drivers are for your organization.

10X Opportunities

10X opportunities are the big ideas that, if properly executed, could increase company revenue by a factor of ten.

Sharing these 10X opportunities as part of the Elite Compass allows everyone in the organization to see them, so when you see them, you can keep them in mind and potentially be involved in helping to lay the groundwork for future growth of the organization.

Core Strengths

Just like every individual, organizations also have strengths and weaknesses. DLP's core strengths are our engaged team members, culture, client base, vision, integrated business model, and elite execution.

Knowing Your Weaknesses

Elite organizations succeed by identifying and correcting weaknesses. These provide an opportunity for growth and advancement. For example, in our most recent compass at DLP, we identified our weaknesses as "too many priorities" and "technology," so we focused on correcting those weaknesses.

Key Numbers

Key numbers are the most important metrics in your organization; success must be clearly defined and tracked so it can be achieved. Individual employees, rather than an entire team, take responsibility for key numbers.

Elite companies know what their key numbers are and, because they measure and track these numbers, achieving the related goals comes down to accountability and execution.

Elite Tools

These are the resources available to the team members in an organization to help them function properly within the Elite Execution System. This book details quite a few tools you'll use to succeed within your organization. As I mentioned earlier, the systems are unique and most likely unfamiliar to those who have not used EES before, but they are crucial to helping you succeed in this environment as well as in building an elite career.

They include EES tools, the Elite Journal, *Building an Elite Organization*, this book, *Building an Elite Career*, the Elite Compass, the Personal Compass, the Executive IDS Summary, Rocks, WIGs, the Meeting Rhythm, and the RREK, to name a few. We will dig into more of these tools in the chapters ahead, and, as we do, you'll be able to see the templates at DLPElite. com/resources.

Keys to Execution

Keys to Execution are the most important activities, improvements, and behaviors that must be accomplished and developed to execute the top priorities in the Elite Compass. Keys to Execution are all the systemic improvements—such as promoting leadership, having a frontline obsession, and driving a great customer experience—that make up the Elite Execution System.

At DLP, our Keys to Execution are Rock Star A Players, Leadership Development, Accountability, Alignment, EES, and the Twenty-Mile March.

Action Steps

- Take time to review your organization's Elite Compass.
- Determine which core value you resonate with the most.
- Pay particular attention to the One-Year Aim and find the areas where you, in your role, can make an impact.

Elite Tip: The One-Year Aim in your organization's Elite Compass is a great place to look to come up with your quarterly goals, which, in EES, we call Rocks. We'll cover Rocks in a later chapter. For now, you can review this section to see where you can make an impact in helping to achieve your company's biggest priorities!

SECTION II

SUCCESS, SIGNIFICANCE, AND HAPPINESS

CHAPTER 3

THE PERSONAL COMPASS

*The greater danger for most of us lies not in setting our aim
too high and falling short, but in setting our aim
too low and achieving our mark.*

—Michelangelo

Elite Organizations know that in order to achieve the company's goals, the company must help team members achieve their own goals. Not just their career or work goals, but also their life goals. This is where the personal compass was born, which is an incredible tool to help you achieve YOUR goals.

You just learned how the Elite Compass provides direction for an organization. Without a clear direction, organizations are typically not successful. Similarly, without clear direction in life, people are typically not successful.

To build an elite career, you must determine what an elite career means to you. Your career should be fully integrated into all areas of your life. Achieving success and living a life of significance and happiness is a choice—a choice to be *committed to* living a life of success, significance, and happiness.

The Personal Compass is designed to help you live fully while leaving a legacy. (A legacy is how you want to be remembered.) As we explain the Personal Compass in this chapter, you can access the Personal Compass template at DLPElite.com/resources to start filling out your own.

Being able to live fully is about forming habits and routines that encompass all areas of your life, what we call the Eight F's of life. The Eight F's of Living Fully are:

Source: DLP Capital

- **Faith** is our spiritual life, how we focus on gratitude and an expectancy of good will from our Creator.
- **Family** is an enduring, healthy connection to those with whom we have a lifetime commitment.

- **Fitness** is a striving toward making our physical bodies the best they can be, which is a gift only we can give ourselves.
- **Friends** are those whom we trust, whose company we enjoy, and with whom we share mutual support.
- **Finances** are not only the way we support ourselves, but also the way we support those we love, whether "those" are people or causes.
- **Freedom** is the ability to choose the highest good; there is physical freedom, which most of us enjoy, time freedom, and financial freedom, to name a few.
- **Fun** is enjoyment and recreation, whether it's reading a book, playing a game, or hiking; fun is a crucial element to life.
- **Fulfillment** is doing that which brings you satisfaction and a sense of purpose.

The Personal Compass begins with you determining your personal core values, mission, and "perfect numbers" of your ideal life. Just like an organization's purpose, your personal purpose is your "why." Along with determining your "why," you will want to determine your "what," which is your mission. Mine is, "I will grow as a servant leader, leveraging my strengths purposefully, passionately, and relentlessly pursuing God-sized goals that make a massive impact on the affordable workforce housing, jobs, generation of wealth, and the happiness crisis while being and improving as the best father and husband I can be."

Next comes your BHAG. In Chapter 2, I covered the BHAG for an organization, but it's just as important to have a Big Hairy Audacious Goal for your personal life and for your family. Be bold and write this down, making it known to everyone who will help bring it to fruition.

One of my favorite parts of the Personal Compass is the question: What do I want to be remembered for? This is the foundation of what you want your legacy to be.

My answer is I want to be most famous in my own home. I want to be remembered as a great servant leader who made a significant impact on many lives with a focus on affordable workforce housing, jobs, generational wealth, and the happiness crisis.

Another one of my favorite parts of the personal compass is the question: What are your perfect life metrics? This might be one of the best places to start when thinking about what's meaningful in your life.

Lloyd Reeb, the cofounder of Halftime Institute, suggests an excellent way to determine your perfect life metrics: Imagine thirty years from now, you are sitting next to somebody; maybe it's somebody you don't know, maybe it's your friend or family member. That person says to you, "Hey, Don, how did the last thirty years of your life go?" What would be the characteristics and components of what happened over those thirty years that would enable you to reply, "Oh, they were absolutely perfect"?

For me to be able to say, "They were absolutely perfect," then I will have

- a deep and growing relationship with my Creator that guides my decisions, focus, and time
- three happy, healthy, adult sons who are living lives with significance and making an impact
- forty-plus years of marriage that brought us closer to each other and the Lord
- physical and mental fitness with the potential to live to 150 years of age
- achieved DLP's BHAG of being one of the Forbes Top 100 private companies, providing housing to one

million people and positively impacting one hundred million lives

- a life spent traveling and exploring and surrounded by natural beauty

Use The Personal Compass to plot a course for where you want you and your legacy to be in one, five, twenty, and even one hundred years in the future. What checkpoints would you want for your life twenty years from now? That is a little harder to think about because anything is possible in twenty years. No matter where you are today, you can be anybody you want and accomplish unbelievable things in twenty years. It's amazing what can be done—and maybe even a little intimidating.

Probably hardest of all to think about is your 100-year checkpoint. I aspire to live to 150, with not just a long lifespan, but a long healthy span. I want to be healthy and vibrant well into my tenth decade.

But even if you are not planning to be here one hundred years from now, what do you want to accomplish? What kind of legacy do you want to leave? What do you want to leave behind for your children and grandchildren? What do you want to leave behind on your business or charitable foundation?

Continuing through the sections of your Personal Compass, you will also delineate who is part of your inner circle, or in other words, who are the people you are going to do life with, who are you going to cherish? You'll list your strengths, weaknesses, and the big opportunities where you think you could drive your 10X results. Next, you will list "My 20 Percent" and "My 4 Percent." This comes from the concept of the 80/20 rule, where 80 percent of the results come from 20 percent of the time, so you should focus your time on your best 20 percent.

When you take that a step further, there is a 64/4 rule that is calculated this way: take the 20 percent of your time that produced 80 percent of your results and apply the same 80/20 principle to it; or, in other words, apply the 80/20 principle to the second degree. You will find that 64 percent of your results come from just 20 percent of your most productive 20 percent of time. That means that just 4 percent of your time is producing nearly two thirds of your results.

To say it another way, 64 percent of your results each week are coming from only a few hours of your time.

This is where you are "the best in the world," so you can focus here to achieve the best results.

Action Steps

Start drafting your personal compass:

- Figure out your core values.
- Determine your mission.
- Decide what you want to be remembered for.
- Identify your perfect life numbers.

Elite Tip: Read *Chase the Lion: If Your Dream Doesn't Scare You, It's Too Small* by Mark Batterson. It will help you figure out your God-sized goals—goals that you normally wouldn't select because you can't achieve them without divine intervention.

CHAPTER 4

FIVE KEYS TO SUCCESS, SIGNIFICANCE, & HAPPINESS

If you want to be happy, set goals that command your thoughts, liberate your energy, and inspire your hope.

—Andrew Carnegie

How do we live lives of success, significance, and happiness? I've spent thousands of hours searching for the answer to this question. I've attended hundreds of events, listened to dozens of personal development speakers, read approximately a thousand books, and held hundreds of conversations with incredibly successful people living lives of significance. After years of research, testing, and validation, I have concluded that there are five keys commitments you must make in order to achieve success, significance, and happiness:

1. Intentionality
2. Purpose
3. Goals

4. Grit
5. Growth Mindset

You could call these five keys, characteristics, or behaviors. You could call them choices because it's within our control to decide if we are going to incorporate these keys into our daily lives, or if we're simply going to react to whatever is most urgent or seems expedient in the moment. I call them "commitments" because you must maintain these behaviors, thoroughly and consistently, over time to produce the results you want in all areas of your life.

Key #1: Intentionality

The first key commitment is intentionality. This is the underpinning to all five. In our current state, humans have never been busier, and the greatest challenge many people feel they face today is time management. We are moving at a faster pace than ever before and somehow fitting increasingly more work and connections and commitments into our jam-packed lives.

Some great thinkers around the topics of time management have concluded that it's not a time management problem; it's a priority management problem. In general, you make time for what you prioritize. It's important to recognize that regardless of what you say your top priorities are, where you spend your time demonstrates what your *actual* top priorities are. That might sound simple, but it's a big revelation for some.

Although people at every age feel that they don't have enough time, the reality is that for most, this is far from the truth.

Author Tim Ferriss says, "Being busy is akin to being sloppy with your time and is a form of laziness."

How can he say that?

He's looking at the statistics. The average American watches 3.1 hours of television per day and spends 2.3 hours on social media per day. That's more than 5 hours a day or roughly 30 percent of our waking hours. Yet we feel we don't have enough time.

It's easy to fill up our time with busy work or reactionary activities. Something we like to say at DLP is, "What's important is rarely urgent, and what's urgent is rarely important." This is significant because we often feel busy when we're tending to things that are urgent, things that come at us every day that we feel we must react to. (We don't have to do anything for our phone to ring, a text to come in, emails to arrive, or for people to walk into our offices. There's stuff coming at us all day, every day.)

And the easiest thing to do—what Ferriss calls the lazy thing to do—is to allow what comes at us to fill up our time. When we take this path, we let other people decide how we spend our time, and in some ways, it's easier. It's easier to respond to emails than it is to do critical thinking, to make big decisions, to work on big projects. It's easier to respond to something that comes at us quickly, taking from the knowledge we already have and solving the problem in a couple of minutes.

It's far more difficult to focus on what's important because the important items require intentional action. My wife cyber-schools our two older boys, Donny and Alex, and she certainly spends her time feeling incredibly busy. She is a full-time mom, full-time housekeeper, full-time teacher to two boys. If I had said to her, "Carla, I need you to take on another responsibility that's going to require hours every day," she would have felt that there's no way she could do so because there was simply not enough time in the day.

Yet we felt called to adopt a baby, made it a priority, and took the steps to prepare for a new child to join our family. We found ourselves waiting with no idea when the call would come. In late 2021, we got the call that baby Jacob was being born, so we rushed to the hospital, and the next day, we took him home. Carla, on top of everything else, was now taking care of an infant. Although certainly a labor of love, it consumed a massive amount of her time, especially during those first six months. She handled the change incredibly well, and I would say she is now even more engaged and doing an even better job as teacher and caretaker of our home while handling the responsibility and the commitment of taking care of Jake.

My wife is living proof that when you decide something is a priority, you can find the time. It just requires you to be more intentional about what you do and to embrace opportunities that help you maximize each hour in the day.

One of the most helpful ways to think about intentionality is applying it across the Eight F's of Living Fully: faith, family, friends, freedom, fun, fulfillment, fitness, and finance. To use a baseball analogy, any time that I'm spending on just *one* of the Eight F's of Living Fully amounts to a single. Hitting a single is a good thing, but I don't want to hit singles. I want to hit doubles and triples and home runs—touching on several of the Eight F's of Living Fully all at the same time.

With intentionality, this is possible. I made the decision months ago that I was going to take a mini sabbatical and chose a time of the year when it was most practical for us to be able to travel as a family, considering our boys' sports commitments and schooling. I scheduled the mini sabbatical around a couple events that I had planned and also coordinated the time around some of my friendships, so I could have a few close friends join us during our month of travel. My wife and I had made a commitment to visit all the national parks, so we also included several of the parks on this trip.

During this special family time, I coached my boys in their playoff flag football game, and then we flew to Texas, Arizona, and Colorado where I spoke at and attended multiple events. We stayed at a ski resort, hiked several national parks, and attended an NBA game with friends. We celebrated my son's tenth birthday and flew home to coach my boys in the championship flag football game before heading to Puerto Rico for a family vacation.

My mini sabbatical was a solid "homerun" because it incorporated five of the Eight F's of Living Fully—family, friends, fitness, freedom, and fulfillment. I was not "checked out" from work, just giving intentional blocks of time to specific activities and practices in my life. It took a lot of planning, preparation, and organization, and there were roadblocks along the way. A virus ran through our family over these sabbatical days, leading to one of us being sick for probably a solid week, and it threw our plans off; but that's part of life, and we adjusted and kept rolling.

I'll say it once again—we all make time for those things we prioritize. And when we're intentional about those priorities—planning and doing *on purpose* and not by *accident*—our time finally becomes our own.

I recommend starting by looking at what your schedule is today and then creating your ideal schedule by building it around your goals and priorities. Remember, the urgent is rarely the important.

Key #2: Purpose

I love the quote, "The two most important days in your life are the day you are born and the day you find out why." An effective way to figure out your "why" or purpose is to use the Personal Compass, which we covered in Chapter 3. Have you set aside some time to complete those action steps? If not, be intentional! Free up your schedule, find a quiet place, and start thinking about your core values, your mission, your legacy, and your perfect numbers. When you're done, share it with others because sharing your purpose—in the form of your Personal

Compass—with those close to you can help you cultivate key supporters. You will be surprised when you start sharing your purpose how many people will step up to help you along the way.

I share my Personal Compass with everyone. I want the people I am doing life with to know my compass and be a part of my journey.

I have heard from so many people how powerful sharing their Personal Compass with their family, friends, and inner circle has been for them.

Purpose also applies on a smaller scale and in a more direct, tangible way in our day-to-day lives as well. It is critical to know what your purpose in life is, but it is also important to know what the purpose is of the meeting you are in. The purpose of the project you are working on. The purpose of the next phone call you are making. Knowing why you are doing what you are doing is critical to getting the results you want.

Key #3: Goals

Before setting goals, it's important to assess where you are starting from. We must start with determining where we are across what we call the Eight F's of life, or how we are doing in Living Fully. You need to know where you are starting from in order to be able to set goals on where you want to go. We have built a powerful and simple tool we call the Life Assessment—which we adapted from Darren Hardy's life assessment tool—that helps people evaluate where they are in just a few minutes.

You simply score yourself across several questions in each of the Eight F's of Living Fully that we introduced in this chapter. Your results will provide you with a chart that shows you how you're doing in each of these eight areas. You can access the template for this assessment at DLPElite.com/resources. After completing the assessment, the Living Fully Wheel-of-Life will indicate your scores from one to ten in each of the eight areas.

We recommend concentrating your goals in the areas where your scores are lowest. (The idea is that people who score a ten in fitness and finance have probably already built some effective habits in those areas.)

After the assessment, it's time to list your goals—both big and small and as many as you can think of—for each area of your life. I think the best approach to this part is to simply let yourself dream. Rather than think through the constructs of what's possible and what resources you have, think about what you truly want to accomplish.

Next, write it down as if you have accomplished it.

For example, if your goal is to have a net worth of $100 million, you would write: I have a net worth of $100 million.

Writing your goals in present tense is a great way to generate excitement and innovation as you think about how you will achieve them. When you have identified goals in each of your lower scoring areas, select eight to ten that you want to focus on in the coming year. These you will add to the Living Fully Dashboard, which is part of your Personal Compass covered in Chapter 3. Remember, each of these top goals for the next year need to be specific, measurable, attainable, relevant, and timely (SMART).

The final step is to determine what you can do today, this week, this quarter, or this year to move closer to these goals. Determining your starting point and knowing what shape your life is in, generally speaking, is essential when embarking on a life of success, significance, and happiness.

Key # 4: Grit

Grit is about working toward the same top-level goal for an extended amount of time. It's vital when taking steps to live a life of success, significance, and happiness.

Angela Duckworth, the author of *Grit* and the famed TED Talk about it, says, "I think *grit* is a great way to define passion . . . not just that you have something you care about. What I mean is that you care about the same ultimate goal in an abiding, loyal, steady way. You are not capricious. Each day you wake up thinking of the questions you fell asleep thinking about."

Grit, in other words, is passion combined with perseverance blended with endurance mixed with commitment.

When you have grit, you are eager to take even the smallest step forward rather than take a step to the side toward some other destination. You place a high value on effort—even higher than on talent and skill—and are willing to put in the work of staying focused on your ultimate goal. Those who don't understand might call your focus obsessive because most of your actions derive their significance from their allegiance to your supreme goal. To those of us who have grit, you simply look like you have your priorities in order.

Like Duckworth, I believe in being consistently pointed in the same direction. That's why I recommend using our Personal Compass tool. What does a compass do? It points you in the right direction. With a compass keeping you on the right heading and a healthy portion of grit—applied daily, weekly, monthly, you get the picture—you are setting yourself up for success, significance, and happiness.

Grit is what separates the most successful people in the world from everybody else. The simple answer to, "How do you become successful?" is that you learn and build grit into your life.

Where are you today when it comes to grit? There's a simple test, which takes just a few minutes, to the grit scale at https://angeladuckworth.com/grit-scale/.

When you understand how powerful grit is, you want to help others build grit into their lives. For those of us who are parents, that starts first and foremost with building grit in our children. To build grit in our children, praise them around the activity or the effort, *not* the final results or the skills or the talent that they have.

Key #5: A Growth Mindset

The final key to success, significance, and happiness is a growth mindset. For a long time, it was believed that a person's abilities were largely predetermined and unchangeable. Today, thanks in part to the studies of Carol Dweck, author of the book *Mindset*, we understand that growth is indeed possible. People can improve on anything in their lives. That is a major shift.

A growth mindset sits in direct opposition to a fixed mindset, which says a person's abilities are largely predetermined and unchangeable. While a person with a fixed mindset can be driven and motivated and might want to be successful, the belief that their abilities are static is likely to lead them to blame others for their setbacks or mistakes or simply give up on their goals. After receiving a mediocre performance evaluation at work, they say, "This is who I am, and there's nothing I can do about it. I work hard. There's nothing else I can do." Or, "My boss just does not appreciate me or does not give me the leadership I need."

A person with a growth mindset might receive the same mediocre evaluation, but they would be more likely to say, "I'd like to identify my weakest areas, work on improving my skills, and learn new skills to meet and exceed my team's expectations at the next evaluation." They ask, "What can I do to get better? How can I improve?"

Recently I interviewed a candidate I was super excited about. He scored a 450 on the cognitive test, which is as high as you can get. He answered forty-one questions correctly, which is tied for the most any candidate has achieved. When I showed him his score in our follow-up interview, he asked, "Can I find out which questions I got wrong?"

He didn't want to gloat about the 450. He wasn't concerned with the forty-one questions he answered correctly. He wanted to know about the twelve he got wrong, so he could improve. I believe that's why he got a cognitive score of 450. He has applied a growth mindset, telling himself that he can learn anything and that anything is possible if he is willing to do the work to grow, learn, and improve.

With a growth mindset, a person is more likely to embrace new challenges and persist when they face obstacles. They welcome and want critical feedback and feel comfortable celebrating others' successes.

The truth is, we all are a mix of fixed and growth mindsets. The first time I read Dweck's *Mindset*, I realized that I had a fixed mindset on cognitive ability. I thought everybody had a fixed cognitive ability and didn't think people could improve. After understanding what Dweck says, I've changed my belief. I now understand that if somebody is willing to put forth the work, they can improve their cognitive ability.

It's possible for even those with a growth mindset to have a fixed mindset in certain areas. That can cause you to reject critical feedback because you're not looking for ways to improve that mindset.

So how do you put yourself into a growth mindset in all areas?

Start by figuring out what triggers you to have a fixed mindset. Be willing to put forth the effort. Anything you're not great at today, put forth the effort to get better. Take risks in the company of others. Be willing to put yourself in situations where you might not know the answer. Be willing to make mistakes, even in front of others, so you can get better.

Finally, own your attitude. Growth mindset means embracing challenges, persisting in the face of setbacks, taking responsibility for your words and actions, and acknowledging that effort is a path toward mastery.

Action Steps

- Take the Life Assessment.
- Complete your Personal Compass.
- Read *Grit* by Angela Duckworth and complete the grit scale at https://angeladuckworth.com/grit-scale/.
- Read *Mindset* by Carol Dweck.

Elite Tip: Know that you can improve any area of your life or learn anything if you are willing to do the hard work and commit to learning.

CHAPTER 5

HABITS, DISCIPLINE, & ACCOUNTABILITY

You'll never change your life until you change something you do daily. The secret of your success is found in your daily routine.

—Darren Hardy

As mentioned in Chapter 1, the Elite Execution System is centered on discipline and putting the habits and tools in place to succeed. To be successful in business and life, you need systems centered around discipline.

In EES, we describe this idea as encompassing disciplined thought, disciplined people, and disciplined action.

DISCIPLINE CENTERED SYSTEMS
You need a system centered around discipline

Disciplined Thought   **Disciplined People**   **Disciplined Action**

Source: DLP Capital

Everyone needs discipline to make any improvement or change until they can build a habit or ritual that takes away the need to think about it anymore because it has become routine. Leaders understand that they must build habits that put them in positions to execute. This does not happen by accident. It takes intentional work. These leaders are deliberate and specific about how they spend their time and about building habits that drive productivity.

Leaders also understand that discipline involves giving up what they want right now for something greater down the road—what they really want. With repetition and focus and sacrifice, they learn to forego short-term gratification to achieve long-term fulfillment and accomplishment.

In Chapter 1, I shared our new definition of accountability from *The Oz Principle*, an incredible book on accountability I have read many times. If you haven't read it, I highly recommend it. If you have read it, I recommend reading it again—at least every few years—because as you grow personally and professionally, your perceptions will grow too.

The Oz Principle shares an imaginary horizontal line as the representation of the separator between the two states of accountability and victimization. Above the line is the state of rising above your circumstances to get the results you want and below the line is the state of falling into the cycle of victimhood, where you can easily become stuck.

Above the Line Thinking

At DLP and the organizations we have trained to be Elite Organizations, we embrace the definition of accountability as an empowered personal choice. We continually demonstrate this form of accountability by asking, "What else can I do to rise above my circumstances and achieve the desired results?"

It takes discipline to apply above-the-line thinking and build it into your daily habits. Someone who simply accepts difficult circumstances and uses them as an excuse to stop working to find a solution is living with a below-the-line mentality. This mindset can easily lead a person to lay the blame elsewhere and never be in a winning position.

Of course, within elite organizations, we do not choose to live below the line and take part in the blame game. Instead, by choosing to be accountable, we take control of our response to our circumstances. Accountability starts with a set of clearly defined results and outcomes, and as we journey forward, we must track and review our progress to continually assess where we are in the process of achieving those results.

According to *The Oz Principle*, there are four key elements of accountability: See It, Own It, Solve It, Do It.TM First, you see the problem or challenge. You take responsibility for it. You review possible solutions, and, finally, you choose and act on the solution. Walking through that process, it's easy to see that accountability is a powerful state.

The Accountability Checklist

A helpful tool from *The Oz Principle* is the Accountability Checklist. When you are operating above the line and living with ownership and accountability, you follow the items on this checklist:

- You invite candid feedback.
- You never want anyone to hide the truth.
- You acknowledge reality, including its challenges.
- You always commit 100 percent to everything you do.
- You own your own circumstances and results, even when they are less than desirable.
- You don't waste time on things you can't influence.
- You recognize when you are dropping below the line and quickly avoid feeling like a victim.
- You delight in the daily opportunity to make things happen.
- You constantly ask the question, "What else can I do to rise above my circumstances to achieve the desired results?"

Issue Solving

In a high growth organization, it is easy to identify or see things that could be better. To see problems and issues throughout the organization. Finding processes, activities, technology, reporting, or other things that are not great is not hard. What is hard, what takes work, what requires stepping up and taking ownership—being accountable is solving these issues.

This requires above the line thinking and avoiding falling into the trap of being below the line. Examples of below the line thinking are people who uses excuses like:

- "I am so busy."
- "No one told me."
- "I do not have time."
- "No one trained me."
- "I don't have enough support."
- "I do not know how to do that."
- "That is not my job."
- "That is just how we've always done it."

Below the line thinkers also take many of these costly shortcuts:

- skipping items on a daily checklist
- procrastinating
- failing to get multiple bids on projects
- failing to write things down
- failing to take detailed notes
- skipping preparation for meetings
- failing to communicate updates to the team
- going through the motions but not doing so with intentionality or purpose

In Elite Organizations, however, identifying issues, bringing forward new ideas to solve issues, and truly owning the results is encouraged. In these organizations, it is recognized that challenges arise frequently and that one of the best ways to address them is to gather input from those with a different perspective. This is reflected in the way issues are solved, and we'll go over that full process in Chapter 10, which covers collaboration.

I love the description of the four kinds of people from *The Oz Principle*:

The Four Kinds of People

People who make it happen.
People who watch it happen.
People who wonder what happened.
People who never knew anything happened.

Which kind of person are you?

Freedom through Schedules and Routines

In his book, *The Ultimate Sales Machine*, Chet Holmes says it is not ideas but rather the pig-headed discipline of implementation day in and day out that is the real key to success. What he means is that your consistency and your focus on building habits are where your results will come from.

Schedules and routines are critically important. By creating a schedule, you can live with intentionality to create the life you desire. It's the daily routines and the daily habits that build upon each other to help you achieve your personal and professional goals. Your consistent, daily activities must be aligned with your overall goals.

The Elite Execution System helps you to stay disciplined and aligned by utilizing tools like Rocks, WIGs, and Alignment, which I will cover in future chapters. These tools help you stay on track for your daily, weekly, monthly, quarterly, and yearly metrics and goals.

The Power of the Elite Journal

Creating a life of success, significance, and happiness does not happen by chance. It takes intentionality and daily focus. One of the best practices you can undertake to remain focused and relieve stress is daily journaling.

The journal we use is the Elite Journal, a tool specifically designed to help Elite Execution System users stay on track and center their thoughts on what is most important. Much more than a typical daily journal or planner where you simply record your thoughts, this journal provides you with the framework to achieve big goals. Through casting a vision for your ideal future, planning the steps to get there, executing with massive daily action, and tracking metrics along the way, the Elite Journal provides you with everything you need to reach success.

The journal is utilized by our team members at DLP Capital, by many of the organizations and individuals we have trained, and by many of our family members, as it helps achieve goals in all aspects of life. While I didn't start out a fan of journaling, I've discovered that it increases productivity, decreases stress, and benefits both the individual and the team. Now I am part of multiple networking groups with billionaires who had never used a tool like this; when they were introduced to the Elite Journal, they shared how powerful and helpful it was for them to focus with intentionality on what's most important.

The Elite Journal is a great way to incorporate the practice of intentionality into your daily life. Mirroring goal designing and the Living Fully Dashboard, it walks you through the process of painting your ideal future picture in ten to twenty-five years, defining where you want to be in three years, and your top goals for the year ahead. From there, you can enter quarterly goals (Rocks) and bi-weekly checkpoints (Milestones).

The weekly pages of the journal provide you with the opportunity to reflect on your top wins and lessons learned as well as focus on how you will live fully in all aspects of your life during that week. The daily and weekly scoreboard allows you to track your key numbers.

Finally, on the daily pages, there's a section for both the morning and the evening. On this page, you can write what you are grateful for, recall your top goals, and record what your top priorities are that day to achieve those goals.

It's these intentional daily habits and practices that keep us on track to achieve long-term goals.

You can find the Elite Journal at DLPElite.com/Journal.

WEEKLY PAGES

TOP WINS LAST WEEK

1. _____
2. _____
3. _____

Celebrate by writing successes

TOP LESSONS LEARNED LAST WEEK / AREAS FOR IMPROVEMENT

1. _____
2. _____
3. _____

Are you "off track" in any areas? How could you improve?

TOP LONG-TERM GOALS / FUTURE VISION

1. _____
2. _____
3. _____

TOP ANNUAL GOALS

The habit of writing these top goals each week will keep them top of mind

1. _____
2. _____
3. _____

QUARTERLY ROCKS

Professional
On Track?

☐ 1. _____
☐ 2. _____
☐ 3. _____

If your milestones are "on track" check the box; if not, focus on how you can get back "on track" this week

Personal
On Track?

☐ 1. _____
☐ 2. _____
☐ 3. _____

Taking time before the week starts to plan your week helps to ensure you are working intentionally on the top actions needed to bring about your results.

HOW I WILL LIVE FULLY IN ALL ASPECTS OF LIFE THIS WEEK

FAITH

FAMILY

FINANCES

> True success comes from working and living intentionally. What will you do to "live fully" in each of these areas?

FITNESS

FRIENDS

FULFILLMENT

> It's the discipline to take daily actions that leads to success. The activity scoreboard will help keep you on track. Fill in your goals at the start of the week and keep track of the results daily

FREEDOM

FUN

DAILY & WEEKLY PERSONAL ACTIVITY SCOREBOARD

KEY NUMBERS & HABITS	WEEKLY GOAL	DAILY NUMBERS							WEEKLY TOTAL
		S	M	T	W	T	F	S	
Mornig Routine	7	1	1	1	1	1	1	1	7
Meditation	6	1	0	1	1	0	1	1	5
Journaling	7	1	0	1	1	1	1	1	6
Number of Prospect Calls	50	0	18	7	12	6	5	0	48
Number of Prospect Meetings	10	0	2	4	0	3	2	0	11
Number of Articles Written	4	0	0	0	2	0	1	0	4
Workout	4	1	0	1	0	1	1	1	5

DAILY PAGES

DATE:

Write the
current date here

DAILY MORNING JOURNAL

ATTITUDE OF GRATITUDE ("I AM GRATEFUL FOR...")

1.

Start your day
on a positive note

2.

3.

MY TOP GOALS

1.

2.

3.

TODAY'S TOP PRIORITIES TO REACH THOSE GOALS

1.

Focusing on the top
priorities and dedicating
time to them will move
you closer to your goals

2.

3.

WHAT AM I STUCK ON? HOW CAN I GET "UNSTUCK" TODAY?

Who do I need to
reach out today to get
unstuck? What can I do
to improve to get back
on track?"

TASKS / NOTES

> *Success is the sum of small efforts, repeated day in and day out.*
> — **Robert Collier**

DAILY SCHEDULE

TASKS / NOTES

5 AM
6
7
8
9
10
11
12
1
2
3
4
5
6
7
8
9 PM

Use this section for your daily schedule as well as notes and actions to take

Take time at the end of the day to reflect on what you could have done better, what you are grateful for, and what you accomplished

DAILY EVENING JOURNAL

DAY 1 / WEEK 1

TOP LESSONS LEARNED TODAY / AREAS FOR IMPROVEMENT

ATTITUDE OF GRATITUDE ("I AM GRATEFUL FOR...")

TODAY'S WINS

What were your successes today? Take time to celebrate to end the day in a positive way

Action Steps

- Determine what daily habits and routines you could add to your life to help reach your goals. Update your daily schedule to include times for the routines to make them habits.
- Regularly review the data and track what you expect of yourself.

Elite Tip: Add the Elite Journal to your morning routine and use the daily and weekly personal activity scoreboard to track the key numbers and habits that you defined in Chapter 2 to build the daily habit of focusing on the most important items each day.

BECOMING A ROCK STAR A PLAYER

CHAPTER 6

ROCK STAR A
PLAYERS & THE RREK

*High achievement always takes place in the
framework of high expectation.*

—Charles Kettering

In an elite organization, team members are hired not only because they have the skills necessary for the role but also because they reflect the organization's corporate culture and values. They inspire confidence and have made it clear they are able and willing to perform the job and achieve the expectations. Within organizations utilizing the Elite Execution System, these team members are called Rock Star A Players, and they are the key to an organization's success.

Team members are the fabric that enable an organization to withstand any market cycle and any economic challenge. You are a part of your organization because your leaders believe you are aligned with the values of your organization, possess the needed skill set, and have the capacity to perform at a high level.

The right person embraces the company's core values and expresses these values before hiring. This alignment is something company leaders purposefully seek out in candidates. It's impossible for every talented and hardworking team member to match the core values of every growing company, but it is possible for hiring managers and leaders to have a clear idea of the company's values and to hone their ability to discern when a candidate shares these values.

Hiring team members who share core values and can execute to get the job done is akin to getting the right people onto the bus. Allowing them to move laterally or advance vertically to positions that complement their strengths and skills is getting them into the right seat.

As you utilize the systems and productivity tools used by your company as an elite organization, you will optimize the value you bring and contribute to the growth of the company. This will create opportunities for you to take on new responsibilities, increase the value and impact you have on your organization, and move up within the organization, being rewarded in many ways, including financially.

The EES Hiring Process

Most growing companies have a standard way they go about hiring. When they finally have time, they place a generic ad in a couple of online job sites and get some résumés. Then they find that they cannot dedicate the resources to conducting timely reviews of these résumés, and sometimes they never review them at all.

If they do get around to reviewing the résumés and come across a candidate or two that they like, they rush through the hiring process. They talk to those candidates over the phone and maybe conduct an in-person meet and greet, lobbing a couple of softball questions during the interview such as,

"Are you proficient at solving problems?" and "How do you generally get along with colleagues at work?"

Predictably, they get standard answers such as, "I'm great—a people person!" and "I work really hard!" Already sold by the résumé and their desperate need to get someone on board as soon as possible, they hire the candidate. Basically, the decision to hire the candidate was made before they even conducted the interview, assuming the candidate they interviewed followed reasonable and standard interview protocol.

I fell into this trap myself during DLP's early years, and my company paid the price for it. The amount of time and money spent on choosing the wrong candidate can be staggering. The statistics on this are all over the place, but a conservative estimate, based on my own experiences over dozens of wrong hires, is that you lose $50,000 to $100,000 each time a bad hire doesn't work out.

Not only did I pay the person's salary for weeks (sometimes months or years), but we ended up spending more time trying to figure out how to fix the mistake, all the while suffering from the slowdown the bad hire caused. When the person would leave, either voluntarily or by invitation, the process started all over again.

Fortunately, I spent quite a bit of time refining the hiring process over the years, so I have been able to train other organizations on how to get high performers who are a good match with their company's core values and culture.

The typical search using the EES process takes a minimum of fifty hours, but depending on the role, it could be several hundred hours. Why would a company invest so much time when they clearly are busy and growing fast? It's because their growth rate is *because* they invest so much time in finding Rock Star A Players.

Clarity of Role, Responsibilities, Expectations, and Key Numbers

A key component of this is being intentional in the role of each team member to ensure they are crystal clear on the responsibilities and expectations.

The tool that allows for this clarity is called the RREK, which stands for role, responsibilities, expectations, and key numbers. The RREK defines success for each team member and removes any ambiguity around what their duties will be.

Here's how the RREK breaks down:

- The role is the job description.
- Responsibilities are the actions the team member must perform.
- Expectations are the required results.
- Key numbers are the most important measures of success.

Defining what success is for a role—i.e., the key numbers and expectations achieved—is the first step required before the search for a new team member begins. Let's dive into the components of the RREK in more detail.

Role

The role is a one- to two-sentence overview that describes a position, and the same role can be described in different ways. For example, while one might say the role is "picks up garbage," another might say "cleans up his neighborhood to beautify it and make it a safe place for families to live, play, and work."

When building out the description for a role, ask these questions:

- What does the role do for our clients/customers/ residents/ investors? Why does the job matter to them?
- What makes this team member a superhero?
- How does the job help achieve company purpose?

Responsibilities

Responsibilities are the activities that a team member does in order to achieve the expectations. These activities are necessary in order for the team member to achieve the success defined in the expectations and key numbers. Typically, there are about ten to twenty activities that make up the responsibilities on the RREK.

Expectations

While responsibilities are the actions, the expectations are the results. These are outcomes from taking actions. Questions to ask when building out expectations could include:

- What is the desired outcome?
- How is the desired outcome measured?
- How is that outcome reported?

When expectations are written, they need to be SMART, which stands for specific, measurable, attainable, realistic and time-based. Ideally, there would be about five to ten SMART expectations. Clearly knowing expectations ensures leaders and reports are in alignment on the results that need to be achieved. When it's time for a performance check-in, they should be able to look at the expectations and see clearly if the expectations were achieved or not. You can't create accountability without clearly defining results, and expectations define those results.

Key Numbers

Key numbers are the most important measurable outcomes for the role, as well as for the organization. Each team member should have roughly two to four numbers, and that team member must control the outcome—meaning they are 100 percent responsible for its achievement, and ownership of that key number is not shared with another team member. The buck must stop with them. If it does not, the number needs to be narrowed down or changed.

Action Steps

- If you do not have your RREK, prepare an initial draft of what you believe your responsibilities, expectations, and key numbers are.
- If you have your RREK, review it and determine if it is up-to-date and clearly defines success for your role. Update your RREK as needed.
- Meet with your leader to review and get his or her feedback on your RREK.

Elite Tip: The foundation of building an elite career involves establishing what success is for your role through clear expectations and key numbers and making sure you and your leader are in alignment on what success looks like. Without clearly defined success, it is easy to be incredibly busy but not productive.

CHAPTER 7

DELIVERING *WOW!*

*I've learned that people will forget what you said,
people will forget what you did, but people will never
forget how you make them feel.*

—Maya Angelou

Part of being a Rock star A Player is "delivering WOW" in all that you do.

At DLP, delivering *wow* is so important to us, it's one of our core values. We define it as, "We go above and beyond, delighting and amazing everyone we encounter." It is also part of our Elite Compass and considered one of our brand promises. It is what we deliver to our clients and how we are known.

Delivering wow is about following through on the commitments you make, following up on every client request, responding to calls the same day, following up until the issue is resolved, and not allowing being busy to keep you from getting back to clients; it is about follow-through.

Many companies claim to focus on customer experience (CX), but few give real thought to it. When people consider

CX, they often think about how the customer is treated at the time of the sale, but this mindset is outdated.

The reality is, CX encompasses every way a customer or potential customer interacts with your organization:

- What does your waiting room look like?
- How do you answer the phone?
- How long do you keep clients on hold?
- How easy is it for your client to get the information they need?
- How easy is it for your client to reach someone when in need?

CX is certainly part of the sales process, but it is also the impression an organization makes at every stage throughout the journey. What experience does a customer have when they first see an organization's website? What is the experience when they read the online reviews about the organization? CX emanates from your company's internal culture, and it simply cannot be faked.

Customer experience and employee experience (EX) are closely related. The internal image will always match the external image, regardless of how many inspirational posters or upbeat scripts a company uses. When companies are who they say they are, they deliver wow to both internal team members and external clients and prospects.

In today's market, particularly with the amount of competition most businesses face, this concept is critically important for *all* organizations. Every person in every role can deliver wow in what they do. This is what starts a great team member experience, which, in turn, translates to a great customer experience.

Because DLP has been dedicated to delivering wow for years, we have seen the difference it makes not only in our growth and customer/client relationships but also in job satisfaction among team members. Knowing that what you do matters—and is noticed—is incredibly satisfying. Delivering wow pays dividends in just about every area of business you can think of.

Enthusiastically delivering wow is a habit. Customers get a wow experience when you are proactive about demonstrating a desire for their business. This might mean returning phone calls on the same day or having a space that is secure, well-kept, and has homey, welcoming touches.

The accepted standard is that a dissatisfied customer will speak to ten people, but a pleasant experience won't be shared. Wow is more than a pleasant experience; it's delightful and amazing. When customers and clients experience wow, especially on a regular basis, they become your company's advocates and ambassadors, a mobile marketing team that delivers customized messages, often to those with whom they already have credibility.

Another powerful way these ambassadors deliver enthusiastic referrals is through online reviews. These reviews on online sites are especially influential because companies can't remove negative reviews. They can only address them so that consumers believe they can trust what is posted. Your efforts at delivering wow to customers and clients can result in an online review that is read for years to come.

WOW! Starts Internally

Customer experiences are important, but every single wow experience begins internally, with the team members. The leaders in each department are committed to ensuring each member of their team has a wow experience, from achieving personal goals to advancing their career through a well-defined path.

The Elite Tools are also part of the company's commitment to delivering wow to you. By modeling wow to you, they set a precedent. They equip you with what wow looks like, feels like, and how it is an action created by mindset and supported by framework.

Here are a few ways to deliver wow:

- Focus on creating experiences and moments that are authentic and meaningful.
- Show you genuinely care and build trust with those you encounter.
- Build long-term working relationships, as those are more important than single transactions.
- Smile!
- Have positive enthusiasm in all that you do.
- Go above and beyond what's expected of you.
- Promote the company culture and values.
- Treat others with respect.
- Exceed people's expectations.
- Be kind.
- Follow up with a client after the interaction to make sure their question or concern was fully resolved.
- Make sure every missed call is returned—not just once, but until you have verified the issue or question has been resolved.
- Focus on the frontline.

Frontline Obsession

The frontline obsession concept was popularized in the book *The Founder's Mentality: How to Overcome the Predictable Crises of Growth* by Allen James and Chris Zook. Within the founder's mentality, organizations that effectively manage growth channel those proven strategies and organizational decisions into frontline routines and behaviors. To make this happen, the leaders of these organizations obsess about those operating on the frontline—the workers who deliver wow every day to clients and customers. These frontline team members are seen as heroes as they are the ones delivering critical solutions.

In fast-growth, entrepreneurial organizations, change is constant. When an organization's key leaders are obsessing over the frontline, there is relentless experimentation. Team members are continually using innovative, solution-focused methods to solve problems. As a result, this perpetual experimentation leads to better products, services, and a better customer experience.

To consistently deliver a wow customer experience, there must be a frontline obsession. Everyone must be obsessed with what happens at each point of communication with customers, wherever and whenever that interaction occurs.

What happens at the frontline is critical to an organization's success. Too often, owners and senior leaders lose touch with the nitty-gritty on-the-ground details of how the business is run. They are so far removed from the origin of customer complaints that by the time they get wind of an issue, it's gone through so many layers of messaging and interpretation that all perspectives on the problem have been skewed.

At DLP, we are committed to having our senior leaders stay in touch with the frontline. We expect our leadership team to visit the properties, pick up the phone and answer customer calls, check out any negative online reviews or feedback, and sit alongside their reports to learn how the job is being done. This is not done to check up on the reports, but rather to learn firsthand from the customer, so improvements can be made. There should never be multiple degrees of separation between the information our frontline team members receive and what our senior managers can relate to firsthand.

Having a frontline obsession is simply getting everyone in the trenches working alongside one another. It means all the support coordinators, receptionists, salespeople, and leaders are equally involved in identifying and addressing company problems.

Sticking to chains of command—where, for example, a senior leader talks to a manager who talks to the coordinator and then the coordinator provides information to the manager, who tells the senior leader, who brings it to a meeting—creates, in my experience, inefficiency and costly delays. It fosters a skewed and inaccurate perception of reality.

Customer service should never be considered a lower-rung responsibility. It is *everyone's* responsibility to delight, amaze, and deliver wow to customers and team members every day.

Placing this level of emphasis on the customer experience isn't just something that helps you look a little better or do a better job at reacting to complaints. When you're delivering wow to your customers and you're delivering wow to your team members, you're going to be turning customers into advocates. Advocates come back to you again and again. And that kind of loyalty, it turns out, increases profits in a verifiable and measurable way.

Action Steps

- When you next interact with a customer, ask yourself, "Did I deliver a WOW! experience?" If not, what could you do differently to wow them next time?
- Ask the same question regarding your interactions with fellow team members. Are you wowing them?

Elite Tip: People are attracted to positive energy. If you bring positive energy to each interaction, you will increase your probability of delivering wow exponentially.

CHAPTER 8

ALIGNMENT

*Growth is never mere chance;
it is the result of forces working together*

—James Cash Penney

I t is important to step out of the day-to-day whirlwind and spend time to recalibrate. To make sure what you are doing and how you are spending your time is in alignment with your goals and the goals of your team. It can be very easy to run really hard, working tirelessly for days, weeks, or months, and end up out of alignment and in need of getting realigned. Alignment is the required launching pad for achieving one's short-term, midterm and long-term goals.

In an elite organization, you thrive when you achieve alignment in three key areas: with yourself, with your leader, and with your team.

To be aligned with yourself means connecting what you want to accomplish in life with where you are today, how you spend your time, and any changes you need to make to achieve those goals. In short, aligning how you spend your time with the goals of your personal compass.

Alignment with your leader requires agreement between you and your leader on what success is for your role, i.e., your expectations and key numbers. Once there is agreement and clarity around success, then the next step is evaluation of your performance against the defined success.

Alignment with your team requires a clear understanding of one another's roles and how to best maximize everyone's efforts to achieve the broader goals of the team. In addition, the most aligned teams are aware of each team member's individual role and how that role contributes to the achievement of the team's goals, but are also aware of each team member's personal goals. The most aligned teams share their personal compasses with one another, so they can be a part of each other's successes in all areas of life.

All effective alignment is built upon trust and communication and people genuinely caring about one another. Team members work better together when they trust each other, and honest, open communication is the foundation of that trust. Leaders who spend time on alignment value listening, coaching, training, and issue solving and provide their team members with development opportunities.

There are three elements to how you build or break trust.

1. Tell the Truth: Of course, trust is built on the foundation of always telling the truth.
2. Competency: As a leader, you also need to be competent with the knowledge and ability to see a task through to its successful completion.
3. Follow Through: You also need to do what you say within the time frame that you said you would complete it.

These three elements build trust with your team members, and you can utilize the tools from the Elite Execution System to further develop trust and achieve alignment.

The Elite Execution System offers team members a variety of tools to achieve alignment, and you are invited to download more information about them, as well as our workbooks and templates, from DLPElite.com/resources.

Here is a list of tools built around creating personal alignment:

- **Personal Compass**: As described in Chapter 3, this is designed to help you live fully, while living and leaving a legacy and lays out your mission and vision for the future along with the steps to attain it.
- **Life Assessment**: This is a self-assessment to measure your performance in the Eight F's of Living Fully—faith, family, friends, freedom, fun, fulfillment, fitness, and finance.
- **Goal Setting**: This tool allows you a place to set your goals in each of the Eight F's of Living Fully and then add your most important goals to the Living Fully Dashboard.
- **Living Fully Dashboard**: This tool showcases your top goals for the year and helps you keep track of your progress.
- **Elite Journal**: This journal provides you with daily, weekly, and yearly opportunities to practice intentionality by setting and revising goals, tracking progress, and evaluating overall performance.

These tools are built around team and leader alignment, which is developed through honest communication and regular evaluations and meetings.

Alignment Meetings

It has been said that people join companies, and they leave bosses. I believe this to be true the majority of the time. People are so busy and embroiled in so much day-to-day communication on projects, fighting fires, meetings, and simply dealing with the whirlwind that there is very little time for real alignment and connection between a leader and their report. Even if a leader and their report talk all day, it is critical to take the time to step out of the whirlwind and focus on the alignment report at least once per month.

This is the time where you build relationships and trust, establish accountability, align with responsibilities and expectations, identify areas of improvement, and grow opportunities to develop and achieve goals. In other words, this is where you can make true progress for yourself and your company.

These monthly alignment meetings are arguably the most important of all the different kinds of meetings in the Elite Execution System.

Goals of Alignment

Most high-growth organizations consistently struggle with accountability and alignment. The goals of the alignment meetings are to drive accountability and build relationships that will make this accountability—and simply dealing with the day-to-day work challenges—easier and more enjoyable.

Keeping alignment as a priority will help people stick with the company, their role, or a project or priority even when things are hard, they're frustrated, and everything is not going the way they want.

Alignment meetings conducted with passion and genuine care build loyalty and engagement and will drive significant increase in productivity and results.

Alignment Meetings Rhythm

Under the Elite Execution System's alignment meetings rhythm, you will have a total of twelve meetings each year or one meeting per month. Each quarter, these include two monthly huddles, and one alignment GPS meeting.

Monthly Alignment Huddles

The format of an alignment huddle is simple. In this one-on-one meeting with your supervisor, you'll share your personal and professional successes. This is an opportunity to truly get to know each other and for the leader to offer genuine compassion for challenges and excitement for possibilities and successes.

From a leader's perspective, the more the team member shares about their personal lives, the better. This helps build a deeper relationship. During this meeting, you will also report on any to-dos you had on your list from the previous alignment huddle.

The bulk of the time will be spent on solving issues that you bring forward—meaning this is your meeting. It's not a time for your leader to ask you about projects but for you to bring forward issues you'd like to solve.

This huddle will generally last around thirty minutes. You should take time in advance to prepare for these meetings and send your leader the topics you'd like to cover.

Format:
- Successes (5–10 minutes)
- To-Dos (1–5 minutes)
- Issue Solving (20–40 minutes)

Quarterly Alignment GPS (Growth, Progress, Support) Meeting

The format for the full alignment meeting is the same for the alignment huddle, with the addition of a deeper dive into the team member's alignment tools—the RREK, development plan, Personal Compass, Living Fully Dashboard, etc. It includes the following structure.

- Growth
  - Successes & challenges
  - Team member brings forward one growth tool (Personal Compass, Living Fully Dashboard, or development plan).

- Progress
  - Successes & challenges
  - RREK review and alignment
  - Rock setting

- Support
  - Performance check-in conversation, including evaluation of adherence to core values, expectations, and Rocks

This meeting is conducted once per quarter and takes about sixty to ninety minutes. The meeting is designed to be able to dig deep into your growth goals personally and/ or professionally so that your leader can provide advice, encouragement, and direction. In addition, this meeting will make sure there is alignment on what the top priorities are for your role and what success looks like over the next ninety days. Finally, there will be time for you to reflect back over the past ninety days and evaluate your own performance, as well as for your leader to give you clear feedback on your performance so you can continue to improve. It is the leader's job to provide clear, direct, and specific feedback to the team member. As a team member, it is your job to receive that feedback from a growth mindset, with the desire and belief that you can always improve and progress if you are willing to put in the work to learn and grow.

This alignment GPS meeting creates a great opportunity for the leader to provide coaching, guidance, encouragement, and support to the team member. After an alignment GPS meeting, both the team member and leader should be very clear about areas of improvement and focus in order to achieve today's priorities and the next steps to move the team member towards the achievement of his or her long term goals and plans.

Alignment Responsibilities

You have five responsibilities related to the alignment:

1. Invest the time to determine your goals, where you want to go, and why. The tools to do this are the Personal Compass, a development plan with your leader, and your RREK.
2. Review your compass, development plan, and RREK regularly and keep them up-to-date.
3. Fully prepare for the alignment meetings.
4. Remain open and vulnerable.
5. Make sure the alignment meeting is held every month.

It is the responsibility of your leader to do the following:

1. Review your alignment tools fully.
2. Coach and support you.

3. Show genuine care and interest.
4. Provide accountability and clear direction.
5. Make sure the alignment meeting is held every month.

You will notice that it is the responsibility of you and the leader to make sure the meeting is conducted every month. This is because it can be easy to fall out of rhythm and stop doing alignment meetings, sometimes for months. It is especially tempting to skip them when you are busy.

Do not skip them.

Over the long term, conducting alignment meetings demonstrates that you, the team member, are your leader's greatest priority. The only way to achieve incredible results month over month and year over year is through great people who are fully engaged, aligned, and accountable.

Achieving Alignment

Achieving alignment between how you are spending your time and what you want to achieve in your life and in your job is powerful.

Achieving alignment between yourself and your leader is critical to your ability to make the biggest impact and for you to be able to grow and move forward in your organization.

Achieving alignment with your team will lead to great fulfillment and significantly improved outcomes for you and your team.

Action Steps

- Complete and review your RREK, making sure it clearly defines success for your role.
- Complete, review, and update your Personal Compass as needed.

- Schedule your next alignment meeting with your leader, and make sure you and your leader are in alignment on success in your role, as well as where you need to improve.

Elite Tip: Alignment meetings are best done face-to-face; ideally, go on a walk together. Moving or walking together has been proven to help foster more open communication. If you cannot meet face-to-face, then you can still opt to walk separately while on the call together.

CHAPTER 9

COLLABORATION

Alone we can do so little; together we can do so much.

—*Helen Keller*

From the alignment meetings and huddles, you probably have noticed that elite organizations place a high value on collaboration—the true source of a team's power. One of the best examples of collaboration is the effect of a mastermind or a mastermind group. This is a peer-to-peer mentoring group where members solve their challenges with input and advice from the other group members. The concept was coined in 1925 by author Napoleon Hill in his book *The Law of Success* and was further explained in his book *Think and Grow Rich*.

When you bring a challenge to a mastermind group, you get the benefit of different perspectives and the insight of other group members. This energy builds upon itself, allowing you and others to form solutions and devise plans that a single viewpoint could not have created.

Two Heads Are Better Than One

One summary of collaboration is an adage you've heard before: Two heads are better than one. Collaborating offers insight from those with different experiences and skills. Sometimes these colleagues have talents and personalities so different from yours that their viewpoints might never have occurred to you. Because of this, elite organizations require collaboration for most things.

While you'll individually own your Rocks and Milestones, any challenges you have will benefit from collaboration. By relying on your teammates, you'll enjoy the strengths, knowledge, and insight they bring to the table.

Open Communication

You'll need to embrace open communication, even if the advice and feedback are not in line with your beliefs. Collaboration is born of an environment of trust and of influence. It is critical to not make the mistake of thinking of a team member as a competitor. The competitors are outside the organization, not within.

Open communication is essential to effective collaboration. Open communication means treating all ideas suggested during collaboration with respect. It's in these moments of open communication that most of us discover styles that vary greatly from ours can feel uncomfortable. For effective collaboration, remember to be humble and authentic.

Emotional Fortitude

Collaboration requires emotional fortitude, the ability to mentally and emotionally weather setbacks, disappointments, failures, and frustrations. Emotional fortitude consists of authenticity, self-awareness, and self-mastery.

Authenticity is not bluntness. When you are authentic with your leader and team members, you can still be diplomatic and polite. The key is that you express your thoughts and the reasoning behind them. For example, you may believe that an idea a team member has suggested won't improve the situation.

Rather than saying, "That won't work. I've tried it before and that failed," you can authentically express your experience by saying, "When I faced a similar challenge last quarter, we implemented a solution much like you just suggested. We found that we needed a product that offered a more comprehensive mechanism."

Self-awareness is having a clear perception of your strengths, weaknesses, motivation, and emotions and how your approach is impacting others. Self-awareness helps you understand how people perceive your words and actions.

Self-mastery is the ability to control one's own desires and impulses. This is a greater task than self-control; it is being able to reflect only kindness and respect through facial expression, gesture, and conversation while passionately disagreeing. Self-mastery helps keep team members positive about wholeheartedly engaging in collaboration with you to solve the challenges you face.

Emotional fortitude is arguably the most undervalued aspect of human psychology when it comes to training and education, as emotional fortitude is the bedrock upon which we build our psyche.

You'll engage in collaborative activities daily at any of the elite organizations we've trained. These activities include Identify, Discuss, Solve (IDS), Daily Huddles, Pipelines, L10 meetings, and working on various committees. Team members who excel at collaboration are often those who will excel at leadership as the skills necessary to do both will often cross over.

Let's discuss a few of these in greater depth.

Issue Solving with Identify, Discuss, Solve (IDS™)

Issue solving is *solving the issue* by defining exactly what the solution is, what actions are needed to get there, and who will own each action. The solution includes the process that will be used, the ownership and accountability for each part of the process, the tracking that will be used, and a plan for communication throughout the process.

As the team discusses the proposed solution, it can change; but, in the end, the group is left with action items that must be completed. Each of the action items are owned by one person, so everyone knows who is responsible for which actions.

When faced with a challenge—having thought it through and arriving at a couple of solutions (one of which you believe is optimal)—before implementing the solution, review it with your leader in the IDS format. If the challenge continues or escalates, then you'll also present it to your team members.

This may be an issue the team has faced before, and your leader may have some helpful input. Please understand—this discussion won't be seen as a weakness. In fact, one of the ways I come to deeply trust my direct reports is by watching them go through the IDS process. As they explain the solutions they arrived at, and why they think one solution is optimal, I learn how they think, and it builds my trust in their decision-making. It will likely be the same with your leader.

Here is how a typical IDS session works: The leader reviews the list of issues brought forward and prioritizes the top three, always starting with the most important. He or she does not move to the second most important issue until the first issue is solved. In some meetings, you may solve only one issue, and in others you could end up solving many. Regardless, you can consider your IDS meeting to be a success if you focus on your most important issue first. The team member who brought the issue forward should lead the discussion around it.

What is interesting and beneficial about this process is that the issue raised by the team member is not always the issue that needs resolving. The IDS process is an excellent way to get to the bottom of what is really going on. Because so many people are looking at the problem from all angles, the likelihood increases that the collective mind of the group will identify the root issues.

We have a tool that helps you get to the root of the problem and, in turn, its solution much faster. We call it the Elite Executive IDS Summary. This tool can lead to significant breakthroughs; it helps you holistically analyze an issue and lay it out in a format that allows the rest of the team to clearly understand the problem. In addition, the tool helps you think through a proposed solution, including the pros, cons, costs, and action steps needed to implement it. The Elite Executive IDS Summary is available for download on the DLP Elite website at DLPElite.com/resources.

1. Illustration
    a. The 10 Commandments of Issue Solving by Gino Wickman & EOS
        i. Thou Shalt Not Rule by Consensus.
        ii. Thou Shalt Not Be a Weenie.
        iii. Thou Shalt Be Decisive.
        iv. Thou Shalt Not Rely on Secondhand Information.
        v. Thou Shalt Fight for the Greater Good.
        vi. Thou Shalt Not Try to Solve Them All.
        vii. Thou Shalt Live with It, End It, or Change It.
        viii. Thou Shalt Choose Short-Term Pain and Suffering.
        ix. Thou Shalt Enter the Danger.
        x. Thou Shalt Shoot Thy Shot.

Daily Huddles

As the name suggests, these occur every day, and every team member participates in one. Holding huddles first thing in the morning can help energize people and get them into a good mindset. The exact time doesn't matter if you stick to the same time each day; the time that works best is one that coincides with the first hour that all team members are present.

There is no set rule about who belongs in which huddle. You might be included in a huddle that is just your team or even your entire division. They can be held in person or via a video conferencing platform. Huddles can have four or five people or as many as twenty, although in my experience, eight to fifteen people per huddle tends to be the sweet spot.

The purpose of the huddle is to quickly run through what is going on with each person. Each of you will take a turn reporting on your key numbers, your successes, what you are focused on today, and what you might be stuck on. A typical daily huddle will last ten to fifteen minutes.

Let me walk you through a daily huddle using the example of a typical DLP salesperson's huddle report, which will highlight the two most productive tasks that a salesperson engages in—meetings and calls.

"My successes are Dominic invested $500,000, Darrel invested an additional $300,000, and I received a referral from one of our team members, Josh. On the personal front, my Rockets won last night. My first metric is I had one meeting yesterday, and I had twenty-three calls. Today, I'm really focused on bringing in commitments from the event last week, and I'm not stuck on anything today."

The next person, a coordinator on the same team whose job is processing investor paperwork, might say:

"My successes were that we brought in a little over a million dollars in new wire transfers yesterday. Yesterday, I had two IRAs move forward through processing and finalized three signatures for non-IRAs. What I'm focused on today is training a new assistant, and I'm stuck on receiving the accreditation proof from Randy's attorney."

One of the most powerful aspects of the daily huddle is for you and your team members to be able to tout your successes and for the supervisor and fellow team members to recognize the accomplishments. Daily encouragement goes a long way to build teams and drive engagement and productivity. Cheer for your fellow team members when they succeed!

The huddle gives each team member a chance to ask for help if they are stuck on something, as it may be a problem the supervisor or another team member can easily solve. In the example above, for instance, the sales coordinator is stuck on paperwork from an investor's attorney; the salesperson may be able to resolve that quickly with a call to the client.

The huddle also gives supervisors the opportunity to redirect when a team member does not seem to be spending their energy on what is most important to the team or the company. It gives team members a forum in which to engage with their teammates and to communicate with their leader. It allows a leader the opportunity to recognize if a team member is struggling personally or professionally by focusing not only on the information but also on their level of engagement and energy. This doesn't mean the leader will address struggles in that moment; the huddle is designed to be a healthy space where you can be candid.

The normal rhythm of huddles is daily for each small team, with a weekly huddle for the entire company and for specific teams and leadership.

Pipeline Meetings

Pipeline meetings are generally conducted twice a week, and last from about twenty to forty minutes. Pipeline meetings can be incredibly effective to drive revenue & increase efficiency.

The idea is to keep the pipeline—whatever that is and however it works on your team—moving forward. In it, you are accountable for your piece of the process. When everyone knows they're going to have to report on the status of something or someone moving through a pipeline, it is a natural prompt to up their game.

The pipeline meeting helps each team member understand how important their role is in achieving the goal, where they fit in the bigger picture, and finally, establishes stronger accountability.

The composition of the pipeline meeting depends on the size of the organization or division you are part of; if it's relatively small, you'll meet with the entire division twice weekly. But if it's larger, you'll likely break into different pipeline meetings, covering just the portion of the process you are involved with.

The pipeline meeting is designed to help smooth out the processes of business from beginning to end. For these meetings to be as effective as possible, you need to have a pipeline tracker to show you the status of the widget as it moves through the pipeline—for example, moving the client, loan, or potential new team member through the process from x to y.

This is best done using a core business operating system, such as a construction management system, property management system, CRM, investor management system, ATS, or any other workflow/operating system that is used to run your organization. In some cases, an Excel or Google sheet is sufficient.

L10 Meetings

Level 10 Meetings™ (or L10 Meetings) are one of the most critical tools in the Elite Execution System. I learned about Level 10 Meetings from the great Gino Wickman, author of *Traction*. The goal of the Level 10 Meeting is to help you and each of your team members to operate at peak performance, at the highest level, which is a "level ten."

Although we usually run our Level 10 Meetings weekly, some teams hold them biweekly or even monthly, depending on their needs or structure. As a team member of an elite organization, you will have a weekly Level 10 Meeting, and it is an important discipline for the team.

These meetings follow a set format: report on successes, review key numbers and scorecards, review Rocks, update or share news and headlines, and review the to-do lists from previous meetings. Each of these sections should take no more than five minutes. The final part of the Level 10 Meeting—and the most robust and critical—is when you dive into solving concrete issues. We call this Identify, Discuss, and Solve (IDS), introduced earlier in this chapter. This portion of the meeting may run forty-five minutes to an hour or longer.

Report on Successes

Every Level 10 Meeting starts off upbeat, with individual team members sharing about their successes. If you're somewhat introverted, your leader may encourage you to share on specific successes; don't be shy—your teammates want to cheer you on as much as you cheer them on!

Review Key Numbers and Scoreboards

Your team will keep track of key numbers using scoreboards, scorecards, or some other form of tracking, and will use this to let everyone know how the team is performing with respect to your set business goals. If the team is off track, it's important to identify that as early as possible to begin addressing the issue to get back on track.

Review Rocks

Next, each team member will review the team Rocks that they own for that quarter and report on the status of each. If a Milestone is due, they report whether they have accomplished that Milestone or not. If all is going well, they can mark their Rocks as on track. If any are behind, they mark their Rocks as off track. Off-track Rocks become the subject of further discussion during the issue-solving portion of the meeting. We'll dive deeper into Rocks in Chapter 15.

News and Headlines

The news and headlines section is an opportunity for everyone to share whatever is going on in the organization or with individuals that might be of common interest to the group. This might include company news such as new hires or awards, team member accomplishments, or any type of personal news that you may want to share. Your leader will also remind the team of upcoming meetings, events, and deadlines.

Review To-Do Lists

In this section of the meeting, the team looks at the to-do lists that were created in previous meetings. Each individual reports on the status of the to-dos assigned to them, marking them complete when they are done and discussing the status of any outstanding to-dos. If the to-do is not accomplished, it may lead to an issue-solving discussion. When new tasks are assigned in the issue-solving section of the meeting, which we cover next, they must be added to the to-do list to provide accountability regarding the completion of the task.

Types of Level 10 Meetings

At DLP, we have a weekly Level 10 Meeting for each business unit or division. In addition, we have Level 10 Meetings for different focuses, such as "shared function" meetings that we do less frequently, perhaps on a biweekly or monthly recurring schedule.

Action Steps

- Make sure you are part of the daily huddle with your team and bring positive enthusiasm to the huddle.
- Prepare for your next L10 Meeting by suggesting an IDS topic along with its proposed solution.

Elite Tip: Use the Executive IDS Summary to solve issues, both personal or professional. By taking the time to write out a proposed solution, you often end up solving issues simply by applying focused time to the issue you want to solve.

CHAPTER 10

WORLD-CLASS LEADERSHIP

Good leaders always make things happen.

—John Maxwell

Elite organizations are routinely and systematically developing leaders so there is a surplus of people ready for the next opportunity or challenge that comes up as the company grows.

As you work on developing the skills to grow as a leader, you will start to see a change in behavior from the people around you. You will find that they are eager for someone to follow and that they expect you to lead. They will seek you out for help and advice, and this can produce its own set of new pressures. The good news is that one of the perks of becoming a great leader is that you can begin to share your responsibilities with those you nurture into leadership roles.

Since leadership is frequently a core value in the organizations we train, we have deliberately sought balanced, insightful leadership development.

At DLP, we've always been dedicated to leadership, and we've always believed in serving others above all other priorities. Therefore, to better articulate this, we've updated one of our core values from "leadership" to "servant leadership" to exemplify that our goal of leadership is to serve. We lead to serve our fellow team members, clients, and communities.

I have read hundreds of books on leadership, including many great ones, but the best book on leadership ever written, in my view, is *The 5 Levels of Leadership: Proven Steps to Maximize Your Potential* by John Maxwell.

The 5 Levels of Leadership reframed the way I think about leadership—and helped me to understand the progression of leadership to the pinnacle of results and respect. Yet the book is clear in also pointing out that levels of leadership are not fixed and may vary depending on who you are leading.

The Five Levels of Leadership

First Level: Position

At this first level of leadership, people follow you because they have to. A person finds themselves with the title of leader, and it is up to them whether they will begin developing concrete leadership skills—or not. It's possible for someone at this level not to lead in any real sense of the word. You do not want to stay at level one. It's a place to begin growing as a leader.

Second Level: Permission

In level two, people follow you because they want to. Leaders at this level are laying the foundation of all leadership by building and growing relationships. They have earned respect and can influence others, and those people want to follow this leader.

Third Level: Production

A leader begins influencing a team to accomplish goals together. Maxwell describes this level as the one where the fun begins because everyone starts moving forward in concert. At this level, people follow you because of what you have done for the organization.

Fourth Level: People Development

A leader begins to produce other leaders by investing in them and helping them develop the skills needed to lead. At this level, an organization can accomplish considerably more because it can draw on more qualified leaders. In level four, people follow you because of what you have done for them.

Fifth Level: Pinnacle

Leaders at this level are known and respected for their reputation, and others follow them because of who they are and what they represent. They are actively creating a legacy of developing new leaders and creating opportunities, and they are dedicated to constantly growing their own leadership skills as a leader. Pinnacle leaders are rare because of the effort and the commitment to longevity and self-development that are required to reach this level.

I believe the majority of leaders would consider themselves Level 4 or Level 5 leaders, when the reality is that most have not consistently achieved Level 3. What does it take to be that Level 3 leader? I'll share some of my best takeaways on the topic.

To start with, using DLP Capital as an example, we do a great job of hiring and developing leaders who are positive, supportive, encouraging, and bring a lot of energy and excitement to their positions. That helps these leaders quickly achieve Level 2 leadership because they are liked among colleagues. The natural progression to the next level is put well in this good quote: "People come before production," that is, Level 2 comes before Level 3.

In order to achieve Level 3 leadership, you have to be able to consistently produce with and through your team. People follow you because of what you have accomplished—your production. If you consistently do not produce results, not only will you miss achieving Level 3 leadership but you can also fall back to Level 1 as people get frustrated following lax leadership that does not lead them to the desired results. The best people in an organization will especially be frustrated by such failings, as they want to win. In order to achieve Level 3 leadership, you must consistently produce results.

On that topic, I especially like this quote by Peter Drucker: "There are two types of people in the business community: those who produce results and those who give you reasons why they didn't."

Level 3 leaders feel a heavy weight of responsibility for results, which is a "cost" of effective leadership. Level 1 or Level 2 leaders do not feel this weight, as they are more often "helpers" than owners. They have not taken the responsibility for owning the ultimate goal but are instead helping senior leadership—if the goal is achieved, they will celebrate and be excited, but if the goal is missed, they will rationalize the failure as ultimately out of their control. Great organizations have owners—not helpers in leadership seats. Level 3 leaders never lose sight of the objective or goal, understanding that the achievement of the goal is the number one priority.

Level 3 leaders make tough decisions. To make tough decisions, you must dig deep enough to know what tough or difficult decisions need to be made—and the best correlating courses of action.

Certainly, I know that in order to lead others at increasingly higher levels, you must first hold yourself accountable. That means being able to prioritize—and being prepared to win. You must show up to each meeting prepared, organized, and having done what you committed to prior to the meeting.

While those are some of my thoughts on rising to new levels of effective leadership, at DLP Capital we created the 24 Consistent Practices of Level 3 Leaders.

The 24 Consistent Practices of Highly Productive Leaders

It's simple to say, "Leadership is influence," but what will you actually do as a leader? What can you expect those in leadership to be committed to? Over the years, as I've studied leadership principles from thought Leaders like John Maxwell and Jim Collins, my team and I have identified twenty-four consistent practices of highly productive leaders. It is often a challenge for leaders to grow from level two, Permission, to level 3, Production. It's these twenty-four practices that lead to production. Our leaders regularly evaluate themselves in these practices to see where they need to improve.

The 24 Consistent Practices of Highly Productive Leaders

1. Discipline and Building Habits: Discipline is required to create change. Invest in being disciplined enough to build the habits needed to achieve your goals. Once a habit is built, little discipline is needed.
2. Do More Than You Ask of Others: Put in the time and the hard work yourself.
3. Prioritization: Prioritize and commit to the real action to accomplish top priorities.

4. Make Hard Decisions: Listen to feedback and be decisive in making the big decisions.

I love this quote: "Hard decisions, Easy life. Easy decisions, hard life." Make the hard decisions.

5. Difficult Conversations: Embrace having the difficult conversations, rather than sending emails.
6. Critical Thinking: Take the time to analyze an issue—its pros, cons, and a proposed solution.
7. Accountability and Ownership: Own the results you are expected to achieve: "The buck stops here."
8. Preparation and Organization: Fully prepare for meetings, issues, and discussions in advance.
9. Organization and Action: Take notes during meetings and lay out clear action items with owners.
10. Questioning, Asking Why, Digging Deeper: Question information and opinions. Dig deeper for the root issue.
11. Embracing Conflict and Leading Change: Conflict is needed to make progress. Show how you will make changes.
12. Keeping Focus on Results: Results always matter. Keep pushing forward regardless of obstacles.
13. Positive Enthusiasm: Bring energy and excitement to each interaction. Deliver wow.
14. Aligning: Align how you spend time with your goals, yourself, your leader, and your team.
15. Listening: Not thinking about how to reply, but actively listening to understand.
16. Speak Simply and Directly: "If I had more time, I would have written a shorter letter." Sum this up.
17. Coaching: Invest time in others, asking clear questions to help reach their goals.

18. Teaching: Take the time to instruct, test, evaluate, and provide feedback.
19. Inspection of Expectations: Inspecting what you expect shows you care about the results.
20. Performance Feedback: Provide direct feedback with positivity and honesty on how to improve.
21. Follow Through: Do what you say you are going to do when you said you would do it.
22. Obtaining Buy-In: Involve your team in decision-making, invite feedback and discussion.
23. Collaboration: You need others. Leverage their knowledge, strengths, and insights.
24. Emotional Fortitude: Develop the ability to mentally and emotionally weather setbacks.

Highly productive leaders might not yet be masters in all twenty-four of these consistent practices, but typically they are proficient at many of them and are working on continuous improvement. Improving on these twenty-four leadership practices is the path to driving productivity and becoming a highly effective leader.

Ready to give yourself a baseline evaluation? A copy of this leadership assessment can be found at DLPElite.com/resources. I encourage you to score yourself across these twenty-four practices, determine which practices you can improve upon, and then *put in the work* to create your own road map for even more successful leadership.

Critical Leadership Skills

Four of the most critical skills for an elite world-class leader are relationship building, communication, execution, and decision-making. We will discuss each skill in more depth below.

Relationship Building

In my experience, there are four keys to building great relationships: promise keeping, aggressive listening, being consistently compassionate, and truth telling.

Elite world-class leaders provide positive encouragement, critical and honest feedback, and ongoing coaching. They understand that leadership is about service to others and thinking about others before yourself.

Relationships are built on trust, and to be a great leader you will cultivate trust by acting with humility, by acknowledging your team members as whole persons, and when needed, helping others with their life issues as part of the professional development process. In leadership, the adage, "People do not care how much you know until they know how much you care," always rings true.

Communication

To build relationships, you must be committed to open communication, and that requires you to become proficient in the many forms of communication necessary to lead and influence others. It's a common myth that leaders must be best at giving big, high-energy presentations to major crowds. While certainly an important skill and worth taking the time to develop, a more important skill is being able to effectively communicate one-on-one. Leadership is developed through building relationships, and relationships happen at a person-to-person level. If you're wondering whether introverts can excel at leadership when they don't particularly enjoy talking in front of large groups, the answer is yes.

Three important facets of communication are storytelling, speaking clearly, and acknowledging communication is a two-way street.

Storytelling

We all love to hear stories, so it should come as no surprise that people are much more engaged and usually learn better when information is presented through stories, rather than pure data or a list of facts. Stories appeal to emotions, which makes them much more memorable.

Good leaders—and growing leaders—use stories to deliver a message, make a point, and teach. To learn more about how storytelling enhances communications, I recommend Paul Smith's *Lead with a Story* and *Sell with a Story.*

Speaking Clearly

A great leader must develop the ability to speak clearly and directly, both one-on-one and to a larger audience. I have found that some of the smartest people I know tend to struggle with this because they rely too much on "MBA talk."

A leader must be able to clearly articulate a point or message. Using big words or providing long, detailed instructions will only confuse people or, at the very least, lose their attention. Brevity plays a large role in commanding people's interest and attention. The first time I heard Mark Twain's quote, "If I had more time, I would have written a shorter letter," I knew it rang true. It is harder to deliver a message clearly and concisely than to ramble on. It takes more time to prepare a training, a presentation, or a message that is short and concise than one that is long and scattered.

Communication Takes Two

Finally, I want to mention that elite, world-class leaders know that communication is a two-way street. They encourage critical feedback from their reports and team members so they can continue to grow and improve, including providing forums and real opportunities for team members to express their honest opinions.

Execution

The EES definition of execution is getting things done (GTD). Leaders must consistently get things done directly and through their team. A team will not follow a leader into battle if the leader has consistently come up short. Without the ability to lead a team to achieve goals, the team's confidence will be shaken, and they will not have the same conviction and motivation to achieve the next big goal.

This means the leader's priority is to do what they say they are going to do—*always*. This means holding oneself accountable for results in the same manner as the team members are held accountable for results. This applies not only to being accountable and consistently executing on organizational priorities and projects, but also to executing on the commitments made to individual team members—including commitments to provide them with clear communication and accountability.

Maxwell puts it this way: "Leadership is taking responsibility while others are making excuses." In other words, leaders face the music even when they don't like the tune. Leaders are accountable for results, both good and bad. They set the scene so the team can execute.

Decision Making

Decision-making stems from the ability to think critically. Critical thinkers can see enough of the whole picture to identify the root of a problem and then build a solution. One of the most important jobs of a great leader is to simplify the complex, making it easier for the team to execute.

Leaders assume the burden of making difficult decisions so the people who report to them can do their jobs unencumbered. They give their team members a voice by gathering opinions, insights, and feedback, but they know at the end of the day that they must be willing and able to make the decision.

Remember "Hard decisions, Easy life. Easy decisions, hard life." Make the hard decisions.

Develop an Owner's Mentality

Just as a business owner is not necessarily a great leader, a great leader does not have to be an actual owner. But an elite, world-class leader *does* need to have an owner's mentality. This is an important part of leadership. Effective leaders invest in hiring rock star team players, train them, make the expectations clear, and are consistently involved in the frontline customer experience. Great leaders do not just sit in their comfy office and accept second- or third-hand information. They get out and interact with customers, get into the field, spend time with the frontline team members, shadow, and inspect phone calls and emails between team members and customers.

An owner's mentality is also reflected in an understanding of what is required to be a successful leader. Great leaders support their fellow leaders verbally and through action. There is cooperation, not competition. What affects one leader impacts all leaders. When one leader is trying to solve a problem, deliver a message, or change a habit or process, it is critical that other leaders show support, even if it is not their top priority or if they do not completely agree with the decision or initiative.

We all like our own ideas more than we like the ideas of others. It is easier to be passionate about your idea or initiative than it is to have that same passion for someone else's idea. As CEO in my organization, if I push a new initiative and make it top priority, and then leaders tell their team members, "Don't worry about that," or simply do not show support for the initiative, it will often be dead in the water. This is why leaders must support fellow leaders.

Leadership Resources and Tools

I am constantly studying leadership as I attempt to evolve in my own leadership style and incorporate new insights into my company's growth paradigm.

Although I have lost count of the leadership books I have read over the years, the following eighteen titles have significantly impacted my own journey of becoming an Elite, world-class leader, and I highly recommend each one:

- *The Five Levels of Leadership* by John Maxwell
- *The Coaching Habit* by Michael Stanier
- *Leadership and Self-Deception* by the Arbinger Institute
- *Dare to Lead* by Brené Brown
- *Leaders Made Here* by Mark Miller
- *Lead with a Story* by Paul Smith
- *Leadership Wisdom* by Robin Sharma
- *How to Be a Great Boss* by Gino Wickman
- *The Monk Who Sold His Ferrari* by Robin Sharma
- *The Leader Who Had No Title* by Robin Sharma
- *Leading Change* by John Kotter
- *Decisive: How to Make Better Choices at Life and Work* by Chip Heath
- *Good Leaders Ask Great Questions* by John Maxwell
- *Speak like Churchill, Stand like Lincoln* by James Humes
- *21 Irrefutable Laws of Leadership* by John Maxwell
- *The Trillion Dollar Coach* by Eric Schmidt

- *The Servant* by James C. Hunt
- *The 8 Paradoxes of Leadership*, Tim Ellmore

More information about these titles can be found at DLPElite.com/resources, along with additional leadership tools.

Action Steps

- Complete the 5 Levels of Leadership Assessment from John Maxwell.
- Complete the 24 Consistent Practices of Highly Productive Leaders Assessment (available at DLPElite. com/Resources).

Elite Tip: Know that leaders are not born. You can grow and develop in your leadership. Choose three practices from the twenty-four practices that you would like to improve, and put intentional focus on improving those three over the next month.

SECTION IV

UTILIZING EES TO DRIVE PRODUCTIVITY

CHAPTER 11

THE EIGHT E'S TO ELITE TEAM RESULTS

Coming together is a beginning, staying together is progress,
and working together is success.

—Henry Ford

There are Eight E's to Elite Team Results. You will use these eight keys as a framework as you work within an elite organization to make significant contributions to the organization while taking the steps to live a fully satisfying life.

#1 Expectations—Setting high standards that are clear to the leader, team member, and the entire team

As you learned in Chapter 6, every team member in an elite organization has their RREK, which includes role, responsibilities, expectations, and key numbers. Each team member alone is accountable for achieving those results. In other organizations, you might have been responsible for activities, but elite organizations allow for incredible personal and professional growth by having team members be accountable for results. Again, there's a difference between activity and results.

> Activity (Responsibilities): actions that lead to results
> Results (Expectations): the desired and undesired outcomes of taking actions

These expectations are how your performance will be evaluated. Achievement of these expectations will determine if you should be given more responsibility, opportunities for advancement, raises, bonuses, and more, so set high standards and take the steps to achieve them.

#2 Empowerment—Empowering people to own the outcomes and the path to achieve the outcomes

As Benjamin Disraeli said, "The greatest good you can do for another is not to just share your riches but to reveal to him his own." This is the essence of empowerment. It starts by empowering people to take ownership of their outcomes.

Trust is the foundation for empowering leadership. You build trust when you reveal empathy, logic, and authenticity. This is again why the alignment meetings, covered in Chapter 9, are so important to establishing trust with your fellow team members.

If you want to take on more, have more opportunities to demonstrate ownership, make it known to your leader and team members. Ask them to empower you and give you permission to lead.

#3 Encouragement—Encouraging and coaching people to achieve their goals

Encouragement, which includes coaching, takes time and energy. At first, you might not see tangible, immediate benefits, but this is about investing in others, with the confidence it will pay a return over time. Encouraging others requires that the leader make time for the other person. Coaching needs to be done primarily one-on-one, and it requires commitment by both parties as well as clear goal setting.

A coach asks great questions and listens to the answers. A few great questions to ask, from the book *The Coaching Habit* by Michael Bungay Stanier, include:

- What is on your mind?
- And, what else?
- What's the real challenge here for you?
- What do you want?
- If you say yes to this, what must you say no to?
- What was the most useful or most valuable here for you?

The goal of effective coaching is empowering the team member to find solutions. A coach shouldn't dominate a coaching conversation. Ask the right questions to the other team member to explore the problems and find the solutions. Whether you are being empowered through encouragement and coaching or empowering others through encouragement and coaching, the process and the results are very rewarding.

Even if your leader does not naturally ask you these questions, you can ask them to yourself and tell your leaders the answers. Asking these questions of yourself will bring incredible value, clarity, and alignment.

#4 Experiences—Creating experiences that are unforgettable, epic moments

Experiences are a key to life and a key to thriving teams. We previously covered the importance of delivering wow experiences. To create these wow experiences, focus on creating moments that are authentic and meaningful.

According to *The Power of Moments* by Chip Heath and Dan Heath, one way to create those authentic, meaningful experiences is to spark moments of connection for groups. To do that, you must create shared meaning. That can be accomplished with three strategies:

1. Creating a synchronized moment
2. Inviting shared struggle
3. Connecting to meaning

#5 Energy and Excitement—Bringing positive, high energy to each moment, interaction, and meeting

People are attracted to energy, and energy and excitement are essential to delivering wow. Here are a few things you can do to ensure that you are sharing your energy and excitement:

1. Smile!
2. Cultivate your own energy.
3. Start your day with gratitude.
4. Get your body in motion.
5. Celebrate successes in meetings.
6. Be genuinely excited for those successes.
7. Demonstrate your own passion.
8. Have positive enthusiasm in all that you do.

#6 Engagement—Keeping team members engaged and involved in achieving goals, solving team problems, and making an impact

You and your team will be engaged when your basic needs are met, when you have a chance to contribute, when you have a sense of belonging, and when you have opportunities to learn and grow. Everyone wants to be connected to purpose, mission, goals bigger than themselves—and when they are, they will be engaged.

There are five factors to driving engagement:

- purpose
- development
- a caring manager
- ongoing conversations
- a focus on strengths

What can you do to drive your own engagement and engagement with those on your team?

Attend and **actively participate** in the following:

- Regularly scheduled monthly alignment meetings
- Company-wide training meetings
- Company-wide huddles
- Team meetings
- Company events
- Contests

Leadership is hard. Help your leader by actively being engaged and showing leadership by example.

Complete and use the tools available:

- Personal Compass

- Living Fully Dashboard
- Development Plan
- Elite Journal

#7 Execution—Getting things done by applying intentionality and consistent discipline

One outcome of rapid growth is that unexpected and seemingly urgent concerns will force their way to the top of your priorities. Reacting to these so-called urgent problems can hinder further growth and interfere with execution. These unexpected issues and urgent requests are what I call the whirlwind. The whirlwind is the enemy of execution.

Remember what I shared earlier in the book: "What's important is rarely urgent, and what's urgent is rarely important."

#8 Empathy—Understanding and feeling what others are experiencing from their frame of reference

In the workplace, empathy exists when you and your team members can establish true, empathetic connections with one another, which, in turn, enhances relationships and performance.

The ability to be compassionate and connect with others is critical to our lives, both personally and professionally. To demonstrate empathy, show sincere interest in the needs, hopes, and dreams of others and demonstrate willingness to help them through personal challenges.

The Eight E's to Elite Team Results are powerful individually, but each works synergistically to enhance the other seven. All eight are required for the framework of Elite Organizations and Elite Careers within them.

Action Steps

- Make sure the Expectations in your RREK are clear, SMART, and up-to-date.
- Empower others by asking the right questions, such as, "And what else?" Practice active listening with empathy when they answer.
- Think of one specific event coming up. What is one thing that you can do to deliver wow and make it turn into a truly epic experience?

Elite Tip: To increase engagement, be sure to use the tools and resources available to you that are a part of EES and utilize the alignment meetings to discuss what you learned from these tools and any issues you are having.

CHAPTER 12

PRODUCTIVITY

Time management is an oxymoron. Time is beyond our control,
and the clock keeps ticking regardless of how we lead our lives.
Priority management is the answer to maximizing
the time we have.

—John Maxwell

Those who work in high-growth companies that don't have a system of execution can feel like they are caught up in a whirlwind of nonstop emails, phone calls, and meetings. Is it any wonder that they lose focus and their minds become scattered as they try their best to process the never-ending feeds of information?

Although these people are putting in long hours, most of their time is still spent on matters that do little to directly further the mission of the organization. Unfortunately, more time at work does not usually equal greater productivity. It can be easy to lose sight of the fact that 20 percent of effort drives 80 percent of productivity. It is frustrating to feel like you're spending more time at work while accomplishing less—all at the expense of other areas of your life.

As mentioned before, when describing the "My 20 Percent" section of the Personal Compass, the 80/20 rule, also known as the Pareto principle, states that 80 percent of results come from just 20 percent of actions. The rule applies to pretty much everything. For example, 80 percent of the world's traffic is concentrated on 20 percent of the world's roads; and 80 percent of the world's wealth is controlled by 20 percent of the world's population.

When it comes to individual productivity, 20 percent of a worker's activities produce 80 percent of their results. In other words, for somebody with a forty-hour work week, eight hours of that forty-hour week is producing 80 percent of their results. Even though some people might find it hard to believe that 80 percent of the value they bring to an organization comes from such a proportionately small amount of time, I've personally observed what the studies confirm after working in multiple industries over the course of several years.

Taking this a step further, remember what we covered in Chapter 3, with the 64/4 rule—just 4 percent of your time is producing nearly two-thirds of your results.

The secret weapon part of this discussion comes into focus when you figure out which activities are producing the greatest results. At that point, it's a simple matter of looking for ways to do more of the tasks that reap the greatest rewards.

Consider, for example, if you are part of the company's sales force. The most productive time for sales professionals is when they are engaged either in prospecting for new clients or when they are in front of a customer selling. You would think that sales professionals would spend most of their time engaged in these activities, particularly since all or a significant portion of their compensation is tied to prospecting and selling; however, this is not going to be the case.

The reality is the average sales professional who works fifty hours a week will spend only about two of those hours prospecting and maybe, at best, ten of them at sales appointments. The remaining thirty-eight hours of their week is going to be sucked up by other tasks, such as following up on customer service issues, completing paperwork, and attending meetings, all activities that produce zero sales. As sales professionals start generating a moderate amount of success, they spend less and less time in sales appointments or prospecting and more of their time on this other less productive busy work.

Regardless of your role, the tendency is to get mired in administrative minutiae or caught up in nonproductive day-to-day drills. These tasks present themselves as urgent, as things that you feel you must tackle immediately. Although these so-called urgent tasks are not part of your productive 20 percent, they will hijack your attention, your time, and your focus.

Shifting the Paradigm

Many people feel so burned out, dissatisfied, and disengaged at work and in life that the paradigm must shift; and with the Elite Execution System, it does. The first shift in changing this cycle of being busy-but-not-productive occurs at the organizational level. At DLP, our leaders focus on the Eight F's of Living Fully—faith, family, fitness, friends, finance, freedom, fun, and fulfillment—to be *more* productive at work, even if that means they end up working fewer hours.

Our goal here is to foster what we call work-life integration, where each team member, by integrating all areas of their life, can simultaneously make progress and achieve personal life goals while still progressing in their career. Elite organization leaders embrace and champion you and your team members living full lives.

Before getting into how to bring about work-life integration, I want to acknowledge an important fact. The average American spends more than two hours per day on social media and nearly four hours per day watching television. Everyone has the same amount of time. Most people are not actually overworked, and most do not have a time management problem; instead, they have a priority-management and a lack-of-discipline problem that negatively impacts their productivity.

It requires great discipline and effort, but is possible to achieve work-life integration, and it's significantly easier when you use EES tools to build that discipline into your daily and weekly routines. These tools, available at DLPElite.com/Resources, are designed to help you increase and optimize your productivity. Let's recap a few below:

Life Assessment and Goal Designing (Living Fully Dashboard)

As we covered in previous chapters, the Living Fully Dashboard, which is part of the Personal Compass, is a powerful tool that combines life assessment and goal designing. Completing the life assessment and goal designing exercise is all about living fully. It should be completed at least annually, and many complete it quarterly and track the progress each month. It guides you through an assessment of all areas of your life so that you can set goals that allow you to take control of your time, while designing a life that will make you truly happy, fulfilled, and prosperous.

While it might seem counter-productive to spend time on your personal goals, the reality is that by putting all your focus and energy into working eighty hours a week, you might benefit your organization in the short-term, but sooner or later, your lack of fulfillment in other areas of life will bleed into work, causing all kinds of burnout. This tool encourages you to take control of your life and helps you realize that you can have it all. Real success comes from achieving fulfillment in all the areas of your life that are important to you, not just a few.

The Personal Compass

As explained at length in Chapter 3, this tool helps you connect the dots between your ultimate goals and how you spend your time. Remember to review your compass and make sure you are staying on track. When you are setting your annual and quarterly goals, reference the compass to ensure you are taking the actions you need to achieve your future vision.

Priority Management = Productivity

At the end of the Personal Compass is a section that directly relates to priority management. This section features the habits you will want to start, stop, or continue doing. Examples include going to bed earlier, waking up earlier, reading more, scheduling personal time, and committing to an exercise routine and healthy diet.

Think through what new habits might help add to your success and devise a schedule that accounts for the activities and actions you must take to achieve your goals. This is where the rubber meets the road. Most people who set goals never significantly adjust how they spend their time. To get different results, a person must change their activities. They need to incorporate habits and routines that will move them toward their goals and away from past, lackluster results. This requires not only adding new habits but also breaking old ones. The one thing we cannot create is more time, so when you add something new to your schedule, remove something else.

Once you are confident that you have a schedule that is realistic and will move you toward your goals, it is time to put that schedule into action. This requires adjustments in routines, updating any currently used calendars (such as Google calendar), and then constantly monitoring and adjusting the schedule as needed.

Personal Compass Sharing

Sharing your goals with others adds to your personal accountability and widens your support network. Some leaders might share their Personal Compass with team members, and this level of vulnerability builds stronger relationships.

Personally, I share my Personal Compass with the entire DLP organization. This accomplishes several things. First, the fact that I fully use the tool and keep it up-to-date shows that I walk the walk and really believe in the tool. Second, it helps my team get to know me better and, in turn, builds trust. Third, it serves as an example of how to fully and properly use the tool. I recommend sharing your Personal Compass during Alignment meetings.

Elite Journal

If you have never used a journal before, my guess is the idea of journaling is going to sound time-consuming and possibly silly. You might even discount it as a waste of time. The truth is, daily journaling not only increases productivity but can also help reduce stress, benefiting each team member and the entire organization.

I resisted the idea of journaling for years but have become a true believer in the practice. I have experienced firsthand and witnessed in others how powerful and effective a consistent journaling practice can be to help you stay focused, achieve your goals, and put yourself in a grateful mindset at the beginning and end of each day.

We provide Elite Journals to our team members at DLP, and many of our elite members do the same for the team members at their organizations.

Elite Journals can be purchased on DLPElite.com/Journal.

Leadership Toolbox

The leadership toolbox is a place where leadership resources are organized. This can be a simple Google Drive or Dropbox folder or simply a Google sheet.

At DLP, our leadership toolbox includes a list of our favorite leadership books, past leadership training links, our definition of leadership, and the job of a leader. In short, it is a library of resources to become a better leader. You can access this, along with the other tools at DLPElite.com/Resources.

EES Tools

EES Tools is the productivity software that supports the Elite Execution System by helping you organize your day, week, and quarter for your professional and personal life.

A feature of EES Tools allows you to manage your user profile by adding a photo, selecting when you want to receive email (useful for productivity), and even offers a color-blindness feature for ease of use.

The dashboard allows you to track your Rocks, Milestones, and WIGs, see scorecards and meetings at a glance, and even log into meetings as an attendee or a leader.

You create and customize your workspaces to prioritize what you see. You have the ability to add tiles to your workspace, such as Rocks; and you can toggle Milestones so that they are grouped by date due or by the Rock they are associated with for ease in planning your activity.

The self-updating To-Do list allows you to mark items as complete, and when you do, they disappear from the list. Tracking for L10 meetings is also available on the dashboard.

Productive Issue Solving

One of the best ways to ensure high productivity is to make sure issues are not slowing you down. Bringing forward proposed solutions to the team, solving them, and assigning clear action steps with clear ownership leads to great productivity.

The Power of Fifteen Minutes: Proof Something Brief Can Be Powerful

When trying to get a long list of tasks accomplished—and particularly when we have large projects to complete—it's common to think that we need large blocks of time to work on them. The lack of ability to find large blocks of time to work on these projects can easily lead to the projects or priorities sitting for days, if not weeks, with no movement.

To combat this kind of backlog, I like to apply a concept called "the power of fifteen minutes." It's an idea that demonstrates how dedicating a small amount of time to a task can make a significant impact on your overall productivity. Find a fifteen-minute block in your schedule and devote that time to moving a project forward. No less, no more, and when time is up, move on to another task. You might be surprised at how easy it is to carve out fifteen minutes because these small blocks of time are abundant—waiting for a meeting to start, waiting for an appointment, logged into Zoom but not yet in the meeting room, or even waiting on a client who is running a few minutes behind. Deciding to use these small increments of time to move your day forward has garnered surprisingly productive results for many using the Elite Execution System.

Action Steps

- Define or update your 4 percent in your Personal Compass to determine where you should focus your time for maximum productivity.
- Share your Personal Compass with a friend, colleague, or family member. When you share it, the vision becomes more clear and you are more likely to achieve it.

Elite Tip: While it may not seem obvious at first, the more you adhere to habits, schedules, and routines, the more you will increase your freedom and stay to the schedule to be more productive and achieve more. Taking just five minutes in the morning or the night before to prioritize your most important items for the day reduces stress and leads to greater accomplishment.

CHAPTER 13

THE TWENTY-MILE MARCH

Successful people maintain a positive focus in life
no matter what is going on around them.

—Jack Canfield

We all get caught up in the whirlwind of full email inboxes, to-do lists, interruptions, and distractions that take our focus off of our top priorities. Each of us has the same twenty-four hours in a day, and many times, it seems like the hours we have are not enough. The great news is you can be more focused, more aligned, more organized, more disciplined, and more successful this year than ever before—if you commit to our secret weapon, the Twenty-Mile March.

Jim Collins introduced the concept of the Twenty-Mile March in his book *Great by Choice*. He tells the true story of two expedition crews that set out to be the first ever to reach the South Pole in a harrowing 1,400-mile journey across unknown and treacherous terrain and in temperatures as low as twenty degrees below zero. The team that made it to the South Pole first also made its journey home safely. The other team reached the South Pole thirty-four days later, and tragically, some of its members did not return safely. The difference between these two teams was that the successful team took the Twenty-Mile March approach, marching twenty miles day after day, regardless of the prevailing conditions, and the other unsuccessful team did not, marching forty-plus miles in good conditions and staying in their tents in poor conditions.

After a significant amount of research, Collins concluded that all great companies have one thing in common: adherence to the Twenty-Mile March. The best way for me to explain the Twenty-Mile March is to use the parable Collins shared in his book. By the way, if you're listening to the audio version of this book, I encourage you to find a quiet place where you can sit back, close your eyes, and listen without distraction. If you're driving, please pull over to a safe place, and put your car in park.

Imagine you and a competitor are both standing with your feet in the Pacific Ocean in San Diego, looking inland. You are about to embark on a three thousand mile walk to the tip of Maine. You are both excited and energized to be taking this momentous journey. The challenge is to see who can reach the destination first.

On the first day, you hike twenty miles, making it to the edge of town. You feel pretty good. You pitch your tent, have a meal, settle in, and enjoy a great night's sleep.

On the second day, you march another twenty miles, still enjoying the beautiful weather. On the third day, you march your twenty miles, but now you have reached the heat of the desert. It's stifling, more than 100 degrees, and you feel dehydrated and worn down. You laugh at how people dismiss the harsh desert heat as only a dry heat. It's becoming almost unbearable, and with every step you are fighting the urge to stop and set up camp so you can dive into your tent to get away from the relentless sun. You push through, though, and complete your day's twenty-mile trek. Through sheer determination, you keep up this twenty-mile pace as you make your way through the desert day after day.

Finally, you hit friendlier terrain and cooler weather. The contrast is striking. You feel a surge of renewed energy. The wind is at your back. You know that you are capable of marching many more than twenty miles now, but you stay the course; you hold back; you modulate your pace. You continue your steady march for the rest of your journey, walking precisely twenty miles each day, no more and no less. You push through when the weather is harsh, and you feel grateful when conditions are favorable so you can complete your miles early and rest. You reach Maine a happy and healthy person, rejuvenated from the adventure and with energy to spare.

Now, back to your competitor who was also at the shore of the Pacific Ocean in San Diego with the same trip before him. He has the same equipment as you do, the same map to guide him on his journey, and the same goal of reaching Maine first.

When he embarks on his march, the weather, of course, is also perfect—isn't it always in San Diego? He is excited and energized; he feels on top of the world! He puts in a great effort, completing forty miles on his very first day. He's extremely proud of his progress but understandably exhausted. He pitches his tent, and when he wakes up, the desert is scorching. He lies back down in his cool tent, figuring that because he did such a great job the day before, covering all those extra miles, he might as well hang out in his tent a while longer to avoid the hottest part of the day.

This scenario repeats itself, over and over. On good days, he marches with great enthusiasm till he cannot march anymore. On bad days, he hunkers down in his tent, waiting and whining about how conditions aren't conducive to moving forward.

It's no surprise he has fallen behind. He renews his resolve to pick up the pace. Just before he hits the Colorado high mountains, he finds himself in a stretch of glorious weather.

He goes all out, logging forty- to fifty-mile days to make up for lost ground. Then, while hiking through a particularly perilous patch of terrain, he hits a huge winter snowstorm. He makes it through and finally gets to a spot of relative safety where he can rest for the night. He makes camp and hunkers down. Still traumatized from the experience of navigating that treacherous trail, he decides to stay put until spring arrives.

When spring finally arrives, he emerges physically weakened and psychologically defeated as he stumbles in the direction of Maine. By the time he reaches Kansas City, you, with your relentless, consistent, disciplined twenty-miles-a-day march, have already reached the tip of Maine.

The point of the parable is this: achieving long-term success and maintaining a high-growth and high-profit business year after year requires incredible and consistent discipline, day after day. It means not allowing the conditions or influences of the outside world—whether they concern politics, competition, or the economy, to name just a few—to dictate your decisions or distract you from putting forth relentless disciplined activity, day after day.

When I tell this parable to new team members in our monthly Welcome to DLP meeting, I always ask them, "What is the message of this story?" I usually get a response that goes something like, "Slow and steady wins the race," or "It's the story of the tortoise and the hare."

This response is *partially* accurate. The Twenty-Mile March does rely on consistent effort. But it is much more than that. If you have ever tracked your steps via a step tracking app such as a Fitbit, you can attest to the fact that walking or hiking twenty miles in a single day is a lot of activity; it's a massive amount of activity.

I, and our leadership team at DLP Capital, can personally attest to this. As part of a fundraiser for the Make-a-Wish

Foundation, as a leadership team, we hiked twenty-eight miles in one day. This was a massive amount of activity.

This is the amount of activity I am talking about when I say we adhere to the Twenty-Mile March every day. We engage in massive amounts of activity *every single day.* We don't put forth this level of effort just on good days or on days where we have the time or on the days that we feel like it. The Twenty-Mile March is about everyone in the organization putting forth this level of consistent activity each day, every day. Not just for a week, or a month, but year after year after year.

Becoming a Twenty-Mile Marcher: The 80/20 Rule

To put the Twenty-Mile March into tangible action on the business front, each member of the team must develop their own relentless, consistent focus on marching those twenty miles each day. You'll need to review your quarterly goals (Rocks) and break them down until you can clearly determine the activity level for the month, the week and finally, the day. That daily productivity will equal your Twenty-Mile March.

Interestingly, your twenty-mile focus will be strongly affected by the 80/20 rule mentioned in previous chapters.

Recognizing this as a universal phenomenon in the workplace, in elite organizations such as DLP, team members are trained on the 80/20 principle, fully understanding and embracing the Twenty-Mile March philosophy, and, most importantly, uncovering which tasks produce the personal productive 20 percent.

Because we are very clear about each team member's responsibilities and expectations, we encourage each one to come up with ways to spend more time on the right activities. The results from this approach have been astounding. As mentioned in the last chapter, we are on pace to triple our productivity per person in just a few short years.

The DLP Twenty-Mile March Roadmap to Success

To help our team members better focus their energies on the activities that produce results, we developed the *Twenty-Mile March Roadmap to Success*, which is available on DLPElite. com/resources. It includes twenty-two different ways you can improve your productivity and drastically increase results and achievements. Much of this we have talked about throughout this book already, but the Twenty-Mile March Roadmap is a great way to summarize much of what we have discussed.

1. Have a Purpose.

Do you understand why you do the things you do? Think about what you really want out of life and what you want out of your role in the organization. This is critical. As I said earlier, more than 70 percent of employees today are not engaged at work. If you're not actively engaged in your work, you will not be able to produce consistent growth. You will not be able to live the Twenty-Mile March.

The challenge to have a purpose is best illustrated by "The Lion Chaser Manifesto" taken from Mark Batterson's *Chase the Lion: If Your Dream Doesn't Scare You, It's Too Small*, and it is crucial to the Roadmap to Success. The manifesto reads:

Quit living as if the purpose of life is to arrive safely at death.
Run to the roar. Set God-sized goals. Pursue God-given passions.
Go after a dream that is destined to fail without divine intervention.
Stop pointing out problems. Become part of the solution.
Stop repeating the past. Start creating the future.
Face your fears. Fight for your dreams.
Grab opportunity by the mane and don't let go!
Live like today is the first day and last day of your life.
Burn sinful bridges. Blaze new trails.

Live for the applause of nail-scarred hands.
Don't let what's wrong with you keep you from worshiping what's right with God.
Dare to fail. Dare to be different.
Quit holding out. Quit holding back. Quit running away.

Several DLP team members use this quote as a screensaver or have it taped to their monitors or pinned to their bulletin boards. It seems to resonate with almost everyone as they work to develop greater purpose in their lives and in their work. I hope it resounds in your heart too.

2. Have a Plan and Clear Goals.

One of my favorite quotes by Benjamin Franklin is, "By failing to prepare, you are preparing to fail."

It is important to understand an organization's plan and goals, but it's also important to develop a personal and professional plan and set goals for yourself. This book explains, and DLPElite.com/resources offers, tools and goal-setting exercises to help you evaluate your life as a whole and set clear goals for what you want to accomplish in the long-term, midterm, and short-term.

We recommend that each year you complete a Life Assessment and goal-setting exercise to help you develop your top ten goals for the next year, as well as three- to five-year goals and ten- to twenty-five-year long-term goals.

3. Live Your Company's Core Values.

You were invited to join the team because your values aligned with the company core values. Living out this alignment of values with others who share it is not only productive but also encouraging. When the behaviors and day-to-day actions of each team member align with and drive the core values of the company, productivity cannot help but follow.

4. Achieve Your Rocks and 5. Achieve Your WIGs.

I put numbers four and five, concerning Rocks and WIGs, together here because they will be covered in detail in Chapters 15 and 16. In brief, Rocks are the specific personal and professional goals that each individual sets into motion each quarter, while WIGs are the biggest and most important objectives established collectively by an entire team. Achieving Rocks and WIGs consistently is crucial to succeeding in your role, as it is in growing your business.

6. Increase Your Positivity.

Jon Gordon, in his book *The Energy Bus: 10 Rules to Fuel Your Life, Work, and Team with Positive Energy*, said, "Positive energy is like muscle. The more you use it, the stronger it gets."

I couldn't agree more. The kind of energy you give off makes a remarkable difference to not only your own level of productivity, but also to the behavior of the entire team. Negative energy drags everyone down, whereas positive energy fuels creativity and productivity. When Howard Schultz, the chairman and CEO of Starbucks, was asked how he gets all those baristas to smile so much, he answered, "It's simple. I hire people who like to smile."

Elite organizations don't expect it's possible to take a Debbie Downer and turn that person into a positive individual. Instead, the goal is to hire positive people and then promote the power and importance of positivity within the company, encouraging people to bring their highest energy and most optimistic selves to work each day.

7. Be Accountable.

We apply the definition of accountability set forth in *The Oz Principle* as a personal choice to rise above current circumstances to achieve results. People who view accountability this way are above-the-line thinkers who "See it. Own it. Solve it. Do it."

8. Solve Issues.

This is best explained by the Elite Execution System's use of the IDS method of problem-solving. IDS, covered in detail in Chapter 10, stands for *Identify, Discuss, and Solve.*

9. Continuously Seek Knowledge.

"Driven for greatness," which is interchangeable with "seeking knowledge," is a core value at DLP, and it may be at your elite organization as well. At DLP, we choose a book each month that we read together. These books are on a wide range of topics, such as leadership, productivity, passion, purpose, speaking, storytelling, and habit building. Every other week, we get together to discuss the book in our Driven for Greatness meetings. I know from my own personal experience that getting people to actively expand their knowledge base is a big part of driving productivity.

10. Grow Your Level of Leadership.

As discussed in Chapter 11, leadership is central to success and productivity. When we train other companies to use the Elite Execution System, we focus on elite world-class leadership. We put a tremendous focus on the twenty-four practices of highly productive leaders that are covered in that chapter.

11. Utilize Checklists.

Although encouraging team members to utilize checklists might seem overly simplistic, the fact is that people spend a lot of their time putting thought and energy into routine tasks day in and day out. These are the 80 percent tasks in the 80/20 equation. By putting in place a simple checklist to remind people of these tasks, they are freed up to focus their minds and their energies on the more important jobs at hand. A good checklist is the key to implementing any SOPs.

12. Utilize the Personal Compass.

As mentioned extensively throughout this book, the Personal Compass can help you see where you are going, show the checkpoints to get there, and showcase your top goals on the path to getting there.

13. Have Clear Alignment.

When you have clear alignment with yourself, you are focused on your day-to-day activities, on your long-term goals, and on making sure that you are spending your time building the habits that are going to get you to where you want to go. When you have clear alignment with your team and your leader, you are all on the same page regarding what your individual priorities are and how they fit within the goals of the organization.

14. Build Your Grit.

What the Twenty-Mile March is to organizations, grit is to individuals. Grit is the great differentiator, the secret weapon that separates the greatest, most successful people in the world from everybody else.

Grit author Angela Duckworth defines the term this way: "Enthusiasm is common, and endurance is rare. Grit is passion and perseverance towards long-term goals."

In other words, don't confuse grit with drive and enthusiasm or even skill. Lots of entrepreneurs are very driven and motivated and put tons of energy and time into their businesses, working seventy, eighty, even ninety hours a week. They will have tremendous passion toward a goal *for a short time*. But when the excitement and the newness of constant change get replaced with the mundane aspects of execution, their excitement and energy wane. They look for greener pastures and something else to put their energy and passion and drive into. These people lack grit.

15. Be Obsessed and Hungry.

Actor Will Smith perfectly summed up what it means to be obsessed and hungry when he said, "The only thing that I see that is distinctly different about me is I'm not afraid to die on a treadmill. I will not be outworked, period. You might have more talent than me, you might be smarter than me, you might be sexier than me . . . But if we get on the treadmill together, there's two things: you're getting off first, or I'm going to die."

It is really that simple. If you are willing to hustle the most and outwork the competition, you are going to be the person on top.

16. Build Habits and Do the Activities that Drive Results.

Discipline is giving up what you want right now—short-term happiness and short-term gratification—for what you really want, which is achievement and fulfillment.

Productive people understand that although you need discipline to build a habit, once that habit is in place, you can focus your mind and your energy on improving another aspect of your life or work. It's a chain reaction that begins with building habits through discipline and ends with driving the results you are after.

17. Track Your Progress.

We often hear, "What gets measured gets improved." This sums up the importance of tracking your progress. There are many ways to do that, and in the Elite Execution System, there are several tools ranging from the Living Fully Dashboard in the Personal Compass to the daily and weekly scoreboard in the Elite Journal. I have to say it again: Journaling can be one of the most effective ways to build habits and achieve incredible results.

18. Use the Elite Journal.

As I've shared, the habit of daily journaling increases your productivity, and the Elite Journal was created specifically for those using the Elite Execution System. Many of the team members at DLP and at our Elite member organizations utilize the journal to stay productive.

19. Prospect and Sell.

Are you an accountant? A project manager? A creative team member? Then you may have seen the heading "Prospect and Sell" and figured it had nothing to do with you. But it's important to understand, in an Elite Execution Organization, it is everybody's job to prospect and sell. Everyone in the organization is responsible for driving revenue, not just the sales team. In fact, every interaction with a client, vendor, or partner is an opportunity to prospect and sell. If everyone—from accounting to human resources to legal to operations—takes on the responsibility of driving revenue through prospecting and selling, it's going to lead to a tremendous increase in productivity. Everyone should feel it is their job to help the company find new opportunities and sell the solutions they provide to potential clients and customers. This simple shift in attitude makes a dramatic difference in the ability to drive revenue, which, at the end of the day, is productivity.

20. Stay on Your Twenty-Mile March.

As a team member, you are responsible for maintaining a Twenty-Mile March mindset and following your own Twenty-Mile March best practices. This includes meeting the commitments you make to your teams, tracking progress with each individual and team goal, and using the Twenty-Mile March tools referenced throughout this book. It also entails doing more of the 20 percent of activities and disciplines that will drive consistent results.

21. Preparation.

As I shared before, many have the will to win, but few have the will to prepare to win. Contrary to what a lot of so-called business gurus will tell you, you succeed by doing more, not less. Nobody gets to the top of their game taking shortcuts. You get to the top by doing *more* of the activities that drive results and *less* of the unproductive activities that do not. You must take the 20 percent of your most productive activities and double or triple your time and efforts in relation to those activities, while cutting back on those less productive activities. Do much more of the right things, and you and the company will see exponential growth. You must take the time to prepare to win.

22. Intentionality.

You learned about the importance of Intentionality in Chapter 4, as it is the first of the five keys to success, significance, and happiness. Intentionality happens when you make the choice to act on purpose, not by accident. It also happens when you make time for those things you prioritize. You must intentionally focus your time and your effort on achieving what you desire most in life.

Action Steps

- Think of a process that you often have to manage where there is no checklist. Create a checklist for this process, and share it with those involved in the project.
- Focus on taking the time to prepare for your biggest priorities by preparing for meetings and preparing your schedule to focus on these most important items.

Elite Tip: As mentioned in Chapter 2, at DLP, our Secret Weapon is the Twenty-Mile March. Day after day, week after week, year after year, we keep marching forward, despite the prevailing conditions in the marketplace. This is also key to all great achievements. Keep your primary focus in mind and keep marching toward it every day.

CHAPTER 14

ROCKS

People with clear, written goals accomplish far more in a shorter period of time than people without could ever imagine.

—Brian Tracy

Would you like to accomplish more in just ninety days than you normally accomplish all year? Through Rocks, that is exactly what you will do.

Think of Rocks as your ninety-day world. A Rock is a solid commitment to achieve a particular outcome in a quarter, or ninety days. Rocks are top priorities for the next ninety days that, when accomplished, will move your organization closer to achieving its One-Year Bull's-eye, Three-Year Aim, BHAG, and mission. Before you adopt the discipline of Rocks, it is important to understand what they are *not*.

First, don't fall victim to the trap of enthusiastically setting a bunch of great-sounding goals and calling them Rocks. Rocks are not pie-in-the-sky aspirations or all the dreams you have for the future. Do not approach Rocks with an "it-would-be-great-if-I-could-get-this-done-next-quarter" attitude.

If you consistently miss your Rocks—the inevitable result of reaching too far or being too vague with your short-term goals—you end up significantly undermining your success, as well as the success of your team and the company. These Rocks are what you were hired to accomplish, and they are your primary responsibility.

Second, keep in mind that Rocks are not the responsibilities you already have or the activities that you already engage in on a day-to-day basis. They are not the unanticipated issues that inevitably crop up or the intermittent fires that you must put out simply by virtue of being employed. Rocks are part of a strategic plan. Make sure as you set your rocks each quarter, you look to the goals of the organization—the-one year goals and the organization's 90-day rocks, for direction in what YOU can do in the next 90 days to help the organization achieve the top goals of the quarter. Rocks are the specific, measurable, attainable, relevant, and timely (SMART) goals that are your biggest priorities for the next ninety days.

Each team member that's part of an elite organization will have three professional Rocks and three personal Rocks each quarter. A simple example of how to go about setting Rocks through the most common type of personal Rock people choose: weight loss. If you want to lose weight, you might define your Rock as "I am going to eat better and lose weight." That is not a Rock, however, because it is not SMART. It is not specific and cannot be measured. There is no accountability to achieving the goal as you cannot clearly track if you reached it or not. If you "ate better" but gained weight, did you accomplish the goal? If you lost two pounds, did you achieve the Rock?

A SMART Rock related to weight loss would be, "I am going to lose fifteen pounds this quarter." This is specific, measurable, attainable (presumably, depending on your metabolism and other health factors), relevant, and timely. This is how all Rocks must be set. They must be SMART.

For example, a new property manager at one of DLP's rental communities wanted to improve rent collections. The community she was managing had higher than targeted delinquent rent, and this was the biggest challenge to the community achieving its budget. In her first attempt at setting a Rock, she said, "I am going to get better at collecting rent." This was not a Rock because it was not SMART. There was no way to determine or measure its success.

If she said she was committed to "reducing delinquency by 2 percent by the end of the quarter," that would have been a SMART goal—that is, a Rock (assuming a 2 percent reduction is attainable at this community). This Rock is specific, measurable, relevant, and timely; at the end of the quarter, she can look at her collections and know whether delinquency was lowered by 2 percent or not.

Rocks Are Universal and Personal

For the companies we train on the Elite Execution System, we advise establishing six Rocks a quarter for the overall organization, followed by six Rocks for each team or division.

You and every other team member will have three professional Rocks that will often be in support of the team's Rocks. Therefore, an individual member of the marketing team might set a Rock of increasing their number of social media posts promoting DLP by 50 percent.

Each team member will also have three personal Rocks that have no direct relationship to furthering the goals of the company. The weight loss example mentioned previously is a typical personal Rock. A personal Rock I have established for myself for the current quarter is to have at least twenty-one outdoor activities with my family.

It's very important to note that each Rock has just one owner; Rocks are never shared. So regardless of whether it's a personal Rock, a team Rock, or an overall organizational Rock, one individual owns each Rock; and that one person takes responsibility for achieving that Rock. The team member who owns a team or company Rock counts that Rock as one of their professional Rocks. So, as an example, if you are the head of sales and you own the top organization Rock of "achieving X number of sales," that would be one of your three professional Rocks.

Managing Rocks with Milestones

It can become very easy to get off track toward achieving a Rock without even realizing it. To stay on track, you are going to need a checklist of sorts, and that is where Milestones come into play.

Milestones are the building blocks of Rocks. They are the achievements that you need to accomplish incrementally within the ninety-day period to complete the Rock. Milestones are tracked every two weeks. Your first Milestone is due fifteen days into the quarter, your second Milestone in thirty days, your third Milestone in forty-five days, and so forth. You end up with six Milestones per Rock, with the final Milestone being what must be achieved for the Rock to be accomplished.

The following provides an example of how you would determine a Rock.

Let's say you're a service (maintenance) supervisor at a four-hundred-unit apartment community, and one of your key responsibilities is getting vacated apartments ready for the next resident. Your company goal is to achieve five-day unit turns, which means that when a resident moves out, the vacated unit will be ready to reoccupy within five days. In the industry, this is often referred to as the time it takes to "make ready."

Your current make-ready rate is ten days. As the service supervisor, you know that reducing this timeframe is a huge priority and one of your biggest performance drivers. At the end of Q2, June 30, you establish a Rock to bring the make-ready average in this apartment community down to five days by September 30, the end of Q3.

You're now going to break that Rock down into Milestones:

Milestone one, your first activity-based goal, will be to assess the capabilities of your current vendors and staff—including flooring installer, painters, and cleaners—to name a few—and use what you learn to build a new turnover plan. You set July 15 as the deadline for this Milestone. The new plan you develop to complete Milestone one will lay out specific steps on how to reduce turnover from ten days to five days by the end of Q3.

Milestone two, a results-driven goal, will be to get the turnover average down to eight days. You commit to do this by July 30. Milestone three is to implement pre-move-out inspections where you'll be assessing, before the resident vacates the apartment, what work will be needed to turn over the unit. This system, which will be implemented by August 15, will help you get materials ordered and vendors lined up.

Milestone four is to bring the make-ready average down to six days by the end of August. Milestone five will be to evaluate and tweak, as needed, the new make-ready plan by September 15. And by the time you reach Milestone six, which is to get your make-ready average down to five days by September 30, you will have accomplished your Rock.

Of course, as the service supervisor, you did not meet these Milestones and accomplish this Rock on your own. You needed the support and help of your team—in this example, your three service technicians who report to you.

One of those technicians could own the job of getting each apartment cleaned out—disposing of any leftover resident tenant items, pulling out carpet, demoing damaged kitchen countertops, and so on—so the vendors who need to do the turnover work can get started.

If you have any chance of getting to your five-day unit turnover Rock, this service technician is going to need to speed up the clean-out process. How will he accomplish this? By setting his own Rocks and Milestones, which will play out something like this:

Service technician's Rock: Achieve a one-day prep and clean-out average by September 30.

Milestones to achieve this Rock:

- Milestone one: Clearly measure average unit clean-out time over the first two weeks.
- Milestone two: Implement a clean-out checklist.
- Milestone three: Conduct pre-move-out inspections using the pre-move-out inspection form.
- Milestone four: Complete move-outs for the month on average in three days.
- Milestone five: Conduct pre-move-out inspections at least five days before move-out.
- Milestone six: Complete all September post-move clean-outs in one day.

By following this schedule and meeting his Milestones, this technician will meet his Rock. If, for some reason, he falls behind on a Milestone mid-Rock, he has time to realign and pivot, reset priorities, or rethink processes. If everyone in the company sets Rocks and Milestones like this service technician and his supervisors, the company will steadily make progress toward completing its most important goals.

Milestone to Mission

I've shared how the Elite Compass casts the vision for the organization and the Personal Compass casts the vision for you, the individual in an elite organization. Rocks and Milestones are a key part of achieving the vision defined in the compass.

The Milestones that everyone accomplishes every couple of weeks lead to achieving their Rocks, which, in turn, contribute to the company meeting its overall top Rocks. Quarter after quarter, these Rocks build up until, at the end of the year, the company meets its One-Year Bull's-eye. In three years, the Rocks will have helped the company meet its Three-Year Aim. Hitting bull's-eyes year after year will make it possible to truly live the purpose, achieve the mission, and accomplish the Big Hairy Audacious Goal (BHAG).

By adopting the discipline of Rocks, I can almost guarantee that you will get more done in ninety days than you were formerly able to get done in a year or more. Rocks provide the competitive edge so you can blow past your prior "bests" and achieve incredible results in a shorter time frame than most would think possible.

How to Implement Rocks

Working in a system of Rocks and Milestones requires a certain rhythm, a definite cadence. This is where the discipline of Rock setting comes in.

Defining Rocks

Every quarter, as part of the Elite Execution System, the company defines its Rocks. This is a very open and transparent process that typically begins about thirty days before the end of each quarter. This is also when you start organizing your Rocks.

For DLP and the elite organizations we train, we call this process "The Three Sixes," since each team has six Rocks, each individual has six Rocks—three professional and three personal—and there are six Milestones to meet, one every two weeks, for each Rock.

The first step in establishing the discipline is that the team is committed to doing this—driving it as a focus and a priority—weeks out before the start of the next quarter. To reinforce its importance, setting Rocks will be brought up in nearly every meeting and be a part of nearly every internal company communication. Your Rocks must be set before the beginning of the quarter and they must meet the SMART criteria. You must take time to choose and define your Rocks.

Choosing Rocks can sometimes be a challenge. Leaders of teams will first come up with the team rocks and review those with senior leadership. These rocks can help you in creating your individual professional rocks. I highly encourage you to meet with your leader a few weeks before the beginning of each quarter to collectively develop a good list of potential Rocks, followed by an active and open discussion to determine your rocks.

Before the start of each quarter, team leaders will present their team Rocks to senior leaders. This allows the senior leaders of the organization to review the Rocks, help refine them, ensure they are SMART, and reinforce the company's commitment to accountability. Your company's senior leaders may well be very involved in this process. At DLP, we do this every quarter, and I personally am a part of all Rock presentations, providing engaged, supportive, and critical feedback as needed. We are pros at Rocks at this point and know that they are incredibly important to the continued success of the organization.

Rocks in Progress

Your team leaders will check in with you to track the progress of your Rocks and assess where you are in respect to your Milestones every two weeks. These regular check-ins help you track your achievements as you either mark your Milestones as complete (and your Rock on track) or as not accomplished (marking your Rock as off track). This process continues through the quarter, allowing you to pivot as necessary to get off-track Rocks back on track whenever possible.

Since implementing this system around eight years ago, DLP team members have improved consistently and are now accomplishing approximately 90 percent of their Rocks—up from the 50 percent we were lucky to achieve in the beginning—which has driven the company's very consistent and profitable growth year after year. While the process may seem time consuming, its regular rhythm has proven to produce results for our business, year after year.

Action Steps

- If you have not already, draft your Rocks for next quarter and review them with your leader.
- Review your current rocks and make sure they are on track, and will be at the next Milestone. If they are not, schedule time to focus on getting them back on track.

Elite Tip: One of the best ways to set up Milestones is to alternate between activity-based and results-based Milestones, so you are tracking doing the hard work and achieving the desired results.

CHAPTER 15

WILDLY IMPORTANT GOALS

The more you try to do, the less you actually accomplish.

—Chris McChesney, *The 4 Disciplines of Execution*

In the last chapter, I told you about how incorporating Rocks will help you grow, stretch, and achieve professional and personal goals faster than you ever thought possible. Now I am going to introduce the practice of setting Wildly Important Goals (WIGs), which will propel your team on a path of accelerated growth.

Where Rocks are owned by individuals, WIGs are owned by teams. The WIG concept was first introduced in *The 4 Disciplines of Execution* by Chris McChesney, Jim Huling, and Sean Covey. The four disciplines Covey presented in the book are:

- Discipline One: Focus on the wildly important.
- Discipline Two: Act on the lead measures.
- Discipline Three: Keep a compelling scoreboard.
- Discipline Four: Create a cadence of accountability.

Before I walk through each of these disciplines in detail and explain how they fit into the Elite Execution System's operations quadrant, I want to share an epiphany I had when I first became aware of the WIGs concept.

The Issue with Execution

Every person in a position of responsibility in every fast-growth company in the world has an issue with being reactive, and being reactive interferes with execution.

The faster and larger a company grows, the more often unanticipated matters rear their heads. These constant fires, these never-ending whirlwinds of time-stealing urgency, interfere with everyone's ability to execute.

When you do manage to put out a fire or two long enough to move forward on executing an important goal, you are hit again with a new tsunami of urgent matters that pull you back into reactive mode. It's a cycle that repeats over and over. This scenario is the biggest impediment to execution; and when you stop executing, you stop growing. We can call this the whirlwind.

This is what makes focusing on what is most important so hard; it must be proactive versus all the reactive urgent priorities that come at us each day. If you are going to go out and execute on the tasks that you must do to meet your team's WIGs, you need to put in place a discipline and routine that allows this to happen. You need to step out of the demands of the here and now for a relatively small amount of time so that you can focus on what is wildly important.

This isn't some mystical approach to avoiding having all those urgent priorities and fires that we all must deal with each day in a rapidly growing company. I'm not offering you a magic wand to make them all disappear. There are always going to be urgent priorities that need your attention, and sometimes they will come at you faster and heavier than other times. Implementing WIGs will, however, make sure you are still accomplishing your biggest and most important goals that will lead to consistent and incredible growth—despite the whirlwind—to execute on the matters that promote long-term, consistent, and exponential growth.

Discipline One: Focus on the Wildly Important

The first discipline of execution is to focus on the wildly important. Your leader will sit down with your team and make a list of all the important priorities you want to achieve, and isolate two or three critical priorities that would make the biggest impact on achieving the vision. WIGs are the priorities that, if achieved, will catapult your team forward more than any other.

A WIG is usually a priority the entire team works on, but sometimes there are two WIGs, and one part of the team focuses on the first while the other focuses on the second.

A WIG is achieved through the team's efforts, so it is crucial that every person on a WIG team has a role in moving metrics and a real impact in achieving the WIG. Keep in mind, there will always be more good ideas than the capacity to execute. The team leader will have to prioritize goals. This quote from Apple CEO Tim Cook puts focusing on fewer, rather than every, great ideas:

"[Apple is] the most focused company that I know of, or have ever read of, or have any knowledge of. We say no to good ideas every day. We say no to great ideas in order to keep the amount of things we focus on very small in number so that we can put enormous energy behind the ones we do choose."

Apple has tens of thousands of team members, and they're generating forty billion dollars a year in revenue. Their successful business model—one worth emulating—is to put enormous energy behind a few great ideas.

Once you have been assigned your WIG, pay close attention to where you are, where you want to be, and when you want to be there. In other words, take note of the starting line, the finish line, and the deadline. All WIGs have a finish line in the form of "from *x* to *y* by *when*."

For example, we previously set a WIG for our HR department to fill twenty open seats with Rock Star A Players over a four-month period. We phrased this as: our WIG is to "go from twenty open rock star seats to zero open rock star seats by April 30."

Discipline Two: Act on the Lead Measures

The second discipline to achieving your WIGs is acting on the lead measures.

Lead measures are the actionable leverage points that you control to achieve your end goal. As Archimedes said, "Give me a lever long enough, and a fulcrum on which to place it, and I shall move the world."

Like Archimedes's lever, lead measures are all about being able to achieve a major goal by focusing on moving the point of leverage. In other words, the lead measures are the actionable things you can do today to influence the achievement of your lag measures, the things that tell you whether you accomplished your WIG.

Implementing lead measures must heighten the probability of achieving the WIG. Let's say, for example, you have a goal of losing twenty-five pounds—going from 175 to 150 pounds—in three months. Weighing 150 pounds is your lag measure. The way to achieve the goal is to eat a proper diet with regular exercise. Therefore, lead measures to lose 25 pounds in three months might be (1) number of steps per day, (2) number of strength training workouts per week, (3) number of days per week following the prescribed meal plan. The lead measures are the means of getting to your end goal or lag measure.

We often focus too much on our lag measures—losing twenty-five pounds—without considering how we'll get there. No one can lose twenty-five pounds by simply thinking about it or wishing for it, but you *can* control what you eat, how often you exercise, how many calories you consume and burn. If you focus on managing these lead measures - you'll be able to lose that weight. (I bet you did not expect you would learn the secret to weight loss when you bought this book, did you? In all seriousness, hopefully this simple illustration has convinced you about the importance of lead measures.)

There is no exact right number of lead measures for the achievement of a WIG, but a good range to target is four to eight.

When your leader first sets up the team's WIG, it is vital to determine who participates in achieving that goal. The primary criterion is that each participant must be able to influence at least one lead measure. There's no right or wrong number of people who should be part of a WIG, although there are usually between six and twelve people to keep oversight and accountability manageable.

Returning to the DLP WIG of filling twenty key Rock Star A Player seats, the team undertook several lead measures, or influencing activities, to bring us to our desired result. These included posting job ads, prospecting potential candidates, conducting first interviews, and taking part in panel interviews.

Discipline Three: Keep a Compelling Scoreboard

The third discipline of achieving your WIGs is to keep a compelling scoreboard. This discipline is based on the principle that people play or work much harder when score is being kept.

People like to win. It motivates them. If some neighborhood kids are out playing pickup basketball and you are watching them play, it is very easy to tell if they are keeping score or not. The level of intensity, focus, energy, and effort goes up tremendously when score is being kept. People just play differently when you keep score.

This same mindset happens in business. Without a way to keep score, people don't know if they're making progress or not, if they are doing well, or if they are doing poorly. They don't know if they're achieving the goal or falling short. And even worse, they stop caring. They become disengaged.

To be effective, WIG scoreboards are designed and controlled by you and your teammates. The scoreboard will be highly visible, compelling, and simple to follow. It will reflect accurate lead and lag measures, as well as each WIG team member's score. When looking at the dashboard or the whiteboard or the poster board—whatever the team constructs the scoreboard to be—you and every team member will know exactly where they stand and where each of the other team members stands. It will be easy to see if you are winning or not.

Discipline Four: Create a Cadence of Accountability

Discipline four, create a cadence of accountability, is the discipline of execution. It is all about being accountable for executing on the lead measures that will accomplish your WIG.

The center of this discipline is the WIG session, a short weekly meeting where you and each of your team members report on their own success or failure in meeting the commitments made during the previous week's meeting. The WIG session is held on the same day and time each week and nothing other than the achievement of the WIG is mentioned during the meeting. The entire focus of this meeting is accountability for moving lead measures forward.

Although it may vary according to the size of your organization, a WIG meeting is often led by a rising leader, not necessarily your team leader.

The WIG leader starts off the meeting by succinctly stating the WIG, what progress has been made to date, and whether the group is on track with the WIG. Beginning with the leader, each of you will tell the group the commitments you made the previous week, the results of those commitments, the lead measures that you moved the past week, any lag measures achieved, and whether you are winning regarding your goals. The individual reporting ends with the actual words, "Yes, I am winning," or "No, I am not winning." Then the next team member gets up and does their report.

After all the team members finish reporting on their results, the leader recaps all the lead and lag measures and then makes two or three commitments for what they will accomplish in the coming week. Each team member follows suit, making two to three new commitments, and then the leader adjourns the meeting.

Applying this cadence to those twenty Rock Star A Players we were looking to hire at DLP, a typical meeting around that WIG would go something like this.

Kate, the leader of this WIG, would start off the meeting by saying, "Our WIG is to go from twenty open rock star seats to zero open rock star seat positions by April 30. My commitments this week were to, first, complete three interviews and make two decisions on two key leadership candidates and, second, to review all open key seats and finalize roles with the recruiter. The results of the commitments are that all interviews were complete; drafted career success offers were completed pending final feedback from executives; the key seat review meeting with a recruiter was complete; I conducted two first interviews, one second interview, and completed two career success offers.

Right now, there are six key leader open seats, and in total so far, we've hired fourteen producers, and yes, I am winning."

Jason, our Senior Director of Human Resources, would be up next. "My commitments last week were to get two career success offers out to candidates and to complete new job ads for all open positions. My results are: I actually sent out three career success offers. I posted one new job ad for the only open position I currently have. I had two prospecting calls. I put two candidates into screening. I had four first interviews and three panel interviews. Right now I have three seats that are open, and so far, I've hired two Rock Star A Players. Yes, I am winning."

The next person goes until everyone reports their results. Then each of you will take turns setting the two or three commitments for the next week. This entire process typically takes less than twenty minutes.

When we set the WIG of twenty seats filled, it sounded like an unbelievable number to meet. I'm happy to report that this awesome team succeeded in filling the twenty seats with Rock Star A Players in less than the four months we set for the deadline of the WIG. I have no doubt that if we did not have this WIG, there's no way we would have filled even half of the seats we were after.

Along with the benefits of reaching the goal, you'll discover that an equally exciting benefit of WIGs is the alignment and relationships that get built when team members hold each other accountable. Meeting consistently every week and working together to achieve big goals is a powerful and tremendous team-building tool.

Winning WIGs

Unlike Rocks, which must be accomplished in ninety days, there is no time limit for WIGs. I have been a part of WIGs that are less than three months and WIGS that have taken nearly one year. In my experience, the four- to six-month timeline works best, but it really depends on the nature of the goal.

It's very rare for a team member to achieve 100 percent of their commitments every week. The team will decide what constitutes winning or losing. Typically, that number will hover around 80 percent. Sometimes teams agree to let each member determine what winning means for themselves. The percentage isn't important; what matters is that there is an established and consistent method of accountability and that you are moving toward achieving your WIGs.

When a team member consistently misses their commitments, the leader of that WIG holds them accountable. When I am a WIG leader, I might suggest to the person who is falling short that we follow up offline and talk about how I can be of assistance in getting them back on track. It is critical that each team member contributes their part to winning the WIG. If a team member is not carrying their weight, a decision will have to be made about whether the team member is simply not doing their part, is not clear on what they can do, or is, at the end of the day, the wrong person to be a part of this WIG.

If the team is not making solid progress in achieving the WIG, the leader might hold a problem-solving session to determine what needs to happen to get the WIG on track. Sometimes a team must reconsider the WIG itself. Maybe it is no longer in the team's vision. Maybe the right people are not participating in the WIG, or perhaps the team is just too caught up in the day-to-day whirlwind and needs to regroup, refocus, and remember why this was established as a WIG in the first place.

Action Steps

- If you are not already in a WIG meeting, talk with your leader about joining a WIG where you will contribute by moving the measures weekly, or consider creating your own to accomplish your wildly important goal.
- Make sure your weekly commitments are SMART and you are spending focused time to complete them each week.

Elite Tip: The urgent is rarely important and the important is rarely urgent. By conducting a weekly WIG meeting, you will ensure that you are focusing on the commitments that drive the needle to reach the wildly important goal.

CONCLUSION

Wow, all of this may have sounded like a lot, right?

This is the system that has allowed many organizations to have exponential growth and have team members truly living fully in all aspects of life while contributing to the fast-growth of organizations.

The thought of implementing all the elements of the Elite Execution System at once is going to feel a lot like taking on a giant elephant-sized meal, but don't let that deter you. You don't have to consume every piece of the system at the same time.

What I have tried to provide in these pages is a blueprint, a clear path to travel as you work to create a thriving career and life, so your life is satisfying and fulfilling and makes an impact for generations to come.

Start with determining your personal core values, your purpose, your mission statement, and your BHAG. Get honest about where you are in your growth as a team member and how a lack of discipline might be keeping you from forging ahead.

Review your organization's Elite Compass to see its BHAG, seven-year checkpoint, Three-Year Aim, and One-Year Bull's-eye, and become familiar with your organization's goals through the lenses of the four quadrants—Strategy, People, Operations, and Acceleration.

Begin putting the disciplines in place to make sure you get there: achieving your Rocks and WIGs, solving issues through IDS, aligning with leadership, and engaging throughout your organization by utilizing Alignment, the alignment huddles and meetings to affect your ownership and accountability. Utilizing these tools will build trust and lasting relationships.

All you need to get started is disciplined thought and a commitment to developing a thriving career. Once you are reasonably clear on where you are going, you can truly be a part of an organization filled with other Rock Star A Players who share your core values and want to be a part of achieving a mission that aligns with your personal core values.

If you back up your strategy with disciplined action, you will grow your life and career in ways you can only imagine. You will build a truly great legacy that transcends you, that can and will weather any professional and personal storm.

Keep spreading this disciplined approach to your personal and professional life. Provide a wow experience to your customers, team members, family, and friends, and you will achieve any goals you set for your life and organization. You will likely achieve them faster than you ever thought possible.

It took me more than a decade to build out these tools, refine them, and fully implement them throughout the DLP organizations. If it takes you a year or two or three to get this system fully implemented in your life, you're still way ahead of the game.

Everything you need to get started—implementation guides, training videos, and templates—are available to you at DLPElite.com/resources. In addition, you can subscribe to *Don Wenner's Elite Impact Podcast.*

Building an Elite Career is an amazing ride. Have fun with it as you keep marching that 20-Mile March on your path to greatness.

ACKNOWLEDGMENTS

I would first and foremost like to thank the Lord my Savior for all He has done for me, and the incredible opportunity He has provided to me to serve Him and to show love and use my God-given abilities to achieve God-sized goals that please Him.

I would like to thank my wife, Carla, who has been by my side showing me support, love, and patience over the past twelve plus years. Being married to the CEO of a high-growth business is no easy task; you do it with grace and make life a joy for our children and for me.

I would also like to acknowledge Jim Collins, Lloyd Reeb, Gino Wickman, Verne Harnish, John Maxwell, Sean Covey, Hal Elrod, and Mark Batterson, the great thought leaders who have not only guided my growth but have also been instrumental in the development of the Elite Execution System.

I would like to acknowledge the amazing elite world-class leaders and team members at DLP who have helped develop, test, and improve both the Elite Execution System and the tools we have used over the past decade-plus. I appreciate your patience and willingness to support all the new and consistently evolving set of tools, some of which have turned out to be staples of the Elite Execution System and others that turned out to not work at all.

Finally, I would like to acknowledge the passionate, gritty, driven, positive, relentless, and humble team members who are never satisfied with the status quo, who want to constantly improve themselves and their work so that they can create a bigger impact on the world, in their communities, and for their teams and employers. These elite producers have the discipline, energy, and passion to never give up and never give in. You inspire and motivate me to continue to seek to serve and to give all I can. Thank you.

BIBLIOGRAPHY

Chapter 1

Conners, Roger, Craig Hickman, and Tom Smith. *The Oz Principle: Getting Results Through Individual and Organizational Accountability.* New York: Portfolio, 2004.

Collins, Jim. *Great by Choice: Uncertainty, Chaos, and Luck—Why Some Thrive Despite Them All.* New York: Harper Business, 2011.

Chapter 2

Collins, Jim. *Good to Great: Why Some Companies Make the Leap...and Others Don't.* New York: Harper Business, 2001.

Chapter 3

Batterson, Mark. *Chase the Lion: If Your Dream Doesn't Scare You, It's Too Small.* Colorado Springs: Multnomah, 2016.

Chapter 4

Clifford, Catherine. "Being perpetually busy is a kind of laziness, says '4-Hour Workweek' author Tim Ferriss." *CNBC.com.* August 25, 2015. https://www.cnbc.com/2016/08/25/tim-ferriss-being-perpetually-busy-is-a-kind-of-laziness.html.

Duckworth, Angela. *Grit: The Power of Passion and Perseverance.* New York: Scribner, 2016.

Dweck, Carol. *Mindset: The New Psychology of Success.* New York: Ballantine Books, *2006.*

Chapter 5

Conners, Roger, Craig Hickman, and Tom Smith. *The Oz Principle: Getting Results Through Individual and Organizational Accountability.* New York: Portfolio, 2004.

Holmes, Chet. *The Ultimate Sales Machine: Turbocharge Your Business with Relentless Focus on 12 Key Strategies.* New York: Portfolio, 2007.

Chapter 6

Conners, Roger, Craig Hickman, and Tom Smith. *The Oz Principle: Getting Results Through Individual and Organizational Accountability.* New York: Portfolio, 2004.

Chapter 8

James, Allen and Zook, Chris. *The Founder's Mentality: How to Overcome the Predictable Crises of Growth.* Boston: Harvard Business Review Press, 2016.

Chapter 10

Hill, Napoleon. *Think and Grow Rich.* Meridien: The Ralston University Press, 1937.

Hill, Napoleon. *The Law of Success.* Meridien: The Ralston University Press, 1937.

Chapter 11

Maxwell, John C. *The Five Levels of Leadership: Proven Steps to Maximize Your Potential.* New York: Center Street, 2011.

Chapter 12

Stanier, Michael Bungay. *The Coaching Habit: Say Less, Ask More & Change the Way You Lead Forever.* Toronto: Box of Crayons Press, 2016.

Heath, Chip and Dan Heath. *The Power of Moments: Why Certain Experiences Have Extraordinary Impact.* New York: Simon & Schuster, 2017.

Chapter 14

Collins, Jim. *Great by Choice.* New York: Harper Business, 2011.

Batterson, Mark. *Chase the Lion: If Your Dream Doesn't Scare You, It's Too Small.* Colorado Springs: Multnomah, 2016.

Gordon, John. *The Energy Bus: 10 Rules to Fuel Your Life, Work, and Team with Positive Energy.* Hoboken: John Wiley & Sons, 2007.

Fowler, Curt. "How Starbucks Rocks Their Customers." *Values Driven Results with Curt Fowler.* https://valuesdrivenresults.com/how-starbucks-rocks-their-customers.

Conners, Roger, Craig Hickman, and Tom Smith. *The Oz Principle: Getting Results Through Individual and Organizational Accountability.* New York: Portfolio, 2004.

Duckworth, Angela. *Grit: The Power of Passion and Perseverance.* New York: Scribner, 2016.

Smith, Will. "Not Afraid to Die on a Treadmill." https://www.youtube.com/watch?v=doqS35FfcUE.

Chapter 16

Covey, Sean, Jim Huling, and Chris McChesney. *The 4 Disciplines of Execution: Achieving Your Wildly Important Goals*. New York: Free Press, 2012.

Frommer, Dan. "Apple COO Tim Cook: 'We Have No Interest In Being In The TV Market'." Business Insider. February 23, 2010. https://www.businessinsider.com/live-apple-coo-tim-cook-at-the-goldman-tech-conference-2010-2.

FIGURES/IMAGES

Chapter 1
Illustration of Quadrants

Chapter 2
Growth Flywheel graphic

Chapter 3
Personal Compass Illustration

Chapter 5
Disciplined Thought, People, Action graphic
Elite Journal images

Chapter 10
10 Commandments of Issue Solving

ABOUT THE AUTHOR

Don Wenner is a best-selling author and the founder and CEO of DLP Capital, a private real estate investment and financial services company focused on IMPACTING some of the nation's largest crises through investing in and financing the building of thriving communities that transform lives. DLP has more than $5 billion in assets under management and has been ranked among the Inc. 5000 fastest-growing private companies in the U.S. for 11 consecutive years. Don has closed more than 30,000 real estate transactions totaling over $10 billion. He lives in historic St. Augustine, FL, with his wife Carla and their three sons, Donny, Alex and Jake, and has a mountain home in Asheville, NC.

GET ACCESS

to all of the resources in
BUILDING AN ELITE CAREER at

DLPElite.com/Resources